Can I Ever Be Financially Free? YES!!!

Can I Ever Be Financially Free? YES!!!

A Common Sense Approach to Financial Freedom

Ken Wharram

iUniverse, Inc.
New York Bloomington Shanghai

Can I Ever Be Financially Free? YES!!!
A Common Sense Approach to Financial Freedom

iUniverse books may be ordered through booksellers or by contacting:

iUniverse
1663 Liberty Drive
Bloomington, IN 47403
www.iuniverse.com
1-800-Authors (1-800-288-4677)

Because of the dynamic nature of the Internet, any Web addresses or links contained in this book may have changed since publication and may no longer be valid.

The information, ideas, and suggestions in this book are not intended to render professional advice. Before following any suggestions contained in this book, you should consult your personal accountant or other financial advisor. Neither the author nor the publisher shall be liable or responsible for any loss or damage allegedly arising as a consequence of your use or application of any information or suggestions in this book.

ISBN: 978-0-595-51492-2 (pbk)
ISBN: 978-0-595-61921-4 (ebk)

Printed in the United States of America

Contents

Chapter 1

Procrastination, Financial Independence, and the Eternal Triangle

This book isn't about getting extremely rich in a big hurry. Even Donald Trump couldn't write that one. This book is also *not* about saving money by rewiring your burnt out bulbs and growing your own Rice Krispies. That's a book you wouldn't read. Some other things this book is *not* about include budgeting, manipulating the stock market, life on twenty dollars a day, how to speculate on property starting with no money down, or the joys of futures trading in sow bellies on the Chicago Exchange.

This book is for the average individual. It's about having a healthy awareness of money, what it can do, and what it has to do if you're ever going to be financially independent. If that doesn't seem to be a lofty objective, just consider this: about 90 percent of individuals will never become financially independent. They'll try to work till they die. Or they'll be trying to live on a government pension. Or they'll be dependent on their families.

Only approximately 10 percent will be financially independent. That's important. The average individual can expect to live till about 80. If you retire when you're 60, there's 20 years to consider. And 20 years is a long time to be eating Kraft Dinner.

Especially when you could be having steak occasionally.

This book is also about procrastination. We can all make fairly long lists of things "we're going to start tomorrow." Like the diet. Like getting in shape. Like talking to the kids more. Like starting a savings plan. Like …

1

Like rewriting this book. I successfully put it off for 15 years. (There are people who would argue that I should have put it off longer.) And then I suddenly got upset.

I got upset that people were buying life insurance policies for the wrong reasons. I know one young couple paying way more than they should and not nearly enough coverage.

I got upset that people weren't getting as much payout as they could on their investments. Some people are making 5 percent more on investment than others—and the two investments are equally safe.

I got upset that people were losing thousands by buying the wrong house at the wrong time. I saw a friend who had to walk away from a $26,000 deposit on a home because of that.

I got upset that people were getting in personal trouble because they didn't know how to handle their money. Most marital stress is caused by money problems: ask a marriage counselor.

I got upset and started ranting about all of these things. I was saying something like "Why do the schools teach kids about amoebas when they should be teaching kids stuff like how to buy a house. I mean they're going to spend a lot more time and energy on where they live than on contemplating amoebas." Suddenly I thought to myself, "If you feel that hot about it, why don't you simply sit down and rewrite the book you've been nattering about?" It made me so upset I actually took out my laptop and started.

Then I remembered too how I hate it when people come up and say, "I've got a few words of good advice for you." I usually cringe. You probably do, too. So you'll be doing a lot of cringing though this book, because it does contain good advice. I've seen the advice work. I've seen people with money problems turn their situations around because of the advice that's in here. I've seen people *without* money problems become much better off and achieve financial independence years earlier. So even though you're cringing, you should be paying attention.

And money isn't the only reason you should pay attention.

A few years ago I noticed an important thing about the clients I did financial planning for:

Their financial life is related to how they're doing physically and mentally. If I see somebody chewing their fingernails or under obvious stress, I find that I'm usually right when I guess they're having a financial problem. I started thinking about that—and doodling. And I doodled this triangle:

I call it the Triangle of Life. All three sides—mental, physical, and financial—are supposed to be equal. If you become physically disabled and you don't have the financial resources to see you through, you're going to have problems emotionally. If you have and emotional breakdown, there will be physical and financial side effects.

As a financial advisor, I'm an expert on the financial side of the triangle. I find that if the financial side is in order, it has a stabilizing effect on the other two sides. If you're running into financial pressures month after month, you're not going to feel as well physically or mentally. On the other hand, if you're in good financial shape, you're going to feel better.

That makes the book you're holding as important as a book on exercising, or aerobics, or diet or stress reduction. Because the basic financial planning tools in this book will help with all those other areas.

Children have a charming—and sometimes alarming—way of simplifying complicated concepts. My daughter Andrea who's a teacher came home from school one day and said she instructed her students to stand up in front of her class and explain exactly what their father's did for a living so Andrea gave her students an example of her Dad.

Trying to explain to eight-year-olds the concepts of financial planning seemed pretty difficult to me. She made a few false starts. In the end Andrea explained to her students: "So when people's money gets sick, my Dad makes it well?" "So he's a money doctor," she stated, and then asked her students if they understood. She was confident her kids knew exactly how her Dad was spending his days.

And she was right. But as a money doctor, I find I'm also helping with physical and emotional health too. A story will help prove my point. A young couple contacted me. They were newly married, had just moved into a new apartment and figured they had the world by the tail. He was working as a manager at a local drug store and she was working as a registered nurse. Both were 22, and their combined family income was a healthy $95,000. Rent was modest. And their debts, so they told me, were practically nonexistent.

I started asking questions. Yes, they did have a credit card. Actually they had two—each. And they were all at their limit, which meant they were running a total of $10,000 in debt on each card. They'd bought all the nice toys: the big screen TV, the stereo, the new car, the trip to Jamaica.

And yes, they argued about the debt. Who was going to pay what on which card. Who had enough credit limit to cover the next new toy. They were actually eating out in restaurants using their credit card, because their cash was going towards paying off what they'd charged before. And they were paying 18 percent interest on what they owed.

And the fights were getting worse. So were the headaches.

After we sat down and discussed the situation, I proposed that they take a consolidated loan at the bank and pay off the credit cards. The cost of that loan would be 5-7 percent, instead of the 18 percent the credit card organizations were charging. And there would be one simple monthly payment that could actually be less than the minimum payments they were making now.

Then I asked if they had a pair of scissors. The young lady went to the kitchen and pulled them out of a drawer.

"Do you want to do it, or should I?" I asked.

"Do what?" she asked.

"Cut up the credit cards."

"But we need them."

"Well, you can't use them much because you're at your maximum limits. If you take the bank loan and then start using the cards again, you're going to end up in the same situation again. With the payments. With the fights. With the headaches."

They took turns using the scissors. And the plan—along with some investments in Retirement Plans and insurance—began to work. And with it came better emotional and even physical health.

If the story sounds too simple, take a moment and think of a friend in financial trouble. How is that person's emotional health? How is their physical situation?

As my friend Hoskins would say, "Ulcers don't come free. There's usually a debt behind them." Hoskins is someone you'll be meeting a lot in this book. You'll learn to hate him. I have. I've never had a friend I've hated more. Because he's always right. Which explains why Hoskins is the highest-living miser in Burlington, Ontario.

A word of advice here. Don't try to get through this book all at one sitting. You'll find it easier to take if you take it like medicine: a pill at a time. It's not complicated medicine, it isn't that bad-tasting, but it does go down better a pill at a time.

Chapter 2

Pay Yourself First: Stealth Dollars

I remember an argument many years ago with one of my daughters over her allowance. I don't want to name any names here, but she knows who she is. What the heck—it was Julie.

"HONESTY" in finances is critical.

The allowance in question was five dollars a week so we're going back a few years.

Every Saturday morning I handed over $4.50, waiting for Julie to ask me the question. And on a Saturday in March it finally came.

"Look, my allowance is five dollars, right?" she said.

"Right."

"So how is it that every Saturday I count and I only get $4.50?"

Aha! I'd planned this. This was going to be a valuable illustration of what Daddy did for a living, an example of financial planning and money management. I put on my best Fred MacMurray look, settled back in the chair, and began to explain: "Each week I keep 10 percent out of your allowance."

"Fifty cents."

"Correct!" Yes, the gene pool is a wondrous thing, flowing at full flood. No doubt the clever child had been paying attention as I talked to clients over the phone. The kid was probably also reading my amortization and depreciation tables while I was away, and likely had boned up on government investment instruments.

"So where's the 50 cents?"

"I'm keeping it safe for you."

"Where?"

"If I told you, would it be safe? I mean you might accidentally tell somebody else and they'd tell a burglar and then where would we be?"

"Why are you keeping the 50 cents? It's mine."

"Of course if is. It is also an example of the first rule of financial planning and one of the "Five Laws of Wealth Creation." (We'll talk more about the *other* four laws later in the book.)

"Look, I don't have much time here. Could you get on with it?" (Those aren't the words that came out of her mouth, but that's what her face was saying.)

"One of the first laws of wealth creation and financial planning is *to pay yourself first.*"

"But *you're* paying *you* first—and you're doing it out of my allowance."

"I'm saving it for you. Here's how the rule works. When you get paid, before you pay anybody else, *pay yourself 10 percent first.* Take 10 percent of your salary and hide it from yourself."

"I would, except you've already hidden it."

"And after a while that 10 percent will really pay off. Last time I counted, you'd saved $17.50."

"*You* saved the $17.50. It wasn't my idea."

"Look, if I'd *given* you the extra 50 cents a week, you'd have spent it. And you wouldn't *have* the $17.50. See, if you pay yourself first, you can build up large sums of capital. As it is, you really haven't *missed* the 50 cents a week. If you pretend it's not there, you can't miss it."

"If I had 50 cents I could buy some baseball cards."

"Exactly what I mean. The money would be gone. Vanished. Pfft!"

"Then I could trade my good cards with Anna for some of her traders and then I could go over to Trina's, who'll trade just about anything, and I could end up with even more baseball cards and then I could go to Willie, who'd pay me for the good ones and I'd end up with a loonie."

"Oh?"

"So I figure you owe me about $30 really."

Then again, I figure she takes after my mother's side of the family.

Despite the odd exception, paying yourself first really makes sense. You line up all the bills on the table, but before you pay any of them, you write out a cheque to yourself for 10 percent. And then you put that money in mutual funds, or in bonds, or in your Retirement Plan, or in the bank, or even under a stone. But you hide it from yourself. Money you don't see is money you won't spend.

Hoskins told me how you could prove that to yourself. I was talking to him about laying those interlocking bricks one day and suddenly he told me to turn out all my pockets. As usual, I did what I was told.

In one pocket there were two tens and a two. In the wallet: $70. In the inside pocket of my jacket there was another $20. Total: $121.

"You always carry this much money around on you?"

"About that, yeah," I said.

"You go to the bank and you take out money just to carry it around with you?"

"Yes."

"How much interest is it making in your pockets?"

"Well … none."

"Tell you what. Next time you go to the bank, take out half as much and see what happens."

And I did. And what happened was sort of funny. Where I usually would buy things automatically—a magazine, chocolate bar, golf tees—I started thinking about the little things I bought.

I reported back to Hoskins and told him he'd taught me a valuable lesson.

"What was it?"

"Well, you can cut down an awful lot on the money you spend buying little pieces of junk."

"You missed the main point."

"What's the main point?"

"The main point is that money you can't see is money you don't spend. I call them 'stealth dollars': you can't see them, but they're there. And the more money you don't see the more money you don't spend. And the more money you end up saving and making interest."

It works with pocket money.

And it can work with larger sums.

If you get in the habit of carrying around less, you'll find that after a while you don't miss having it. And if you get in the habit of paying yourself first—10 percent off the top—after a while you won't miss that either. And you'll be building a pile of wealth. (Check the chapters on Retirement Plans and on compound interest to see exactly how much you'd be saving.)

However, the longer you wait to develop the habit, the harder it becomes. That's true because the "10 percent off the top" becomes a larger figure as you start to earn more. Not only that, but you'll have developed some automatic spending habits in the place of the "pay yourself first" habit, and they'll be tough to break.

Almost every financial planning book you can lay your hands on mentions this "pay yourself first" rule. But most people who read financial planning books ignore it. Here's an exercise that'll make it tough to ignore.

My take home pay is: **$50,000.00**
10 percent is: **$5.000.00**
If I invest that at 5 percent interest, according to the Investment Table in chapter six, after 20 years I'll have: **$186,863.00**
Our combined take home pay is: **$95,000.00**
10 percent is: **$9,500.00**

If we invest that at 5 percent interest, according to the table, after 20 years we'll have: **$355,039.00**

That's the reward of paying yourself first. But look at the situation in reverse: the downside of not paying yourself first is that you won't have all those dollars.

You'll have to work for them. Or you'll have to do without.

Neither one of those options is going to make you very happy.

Chapter 3

Being a Millionaire Just Isn't Good Enough Anymore

Hoskins had one of those old-fashioned push mowers. He'd bought the thing—used—instead of taking up jogging. "And it cost less than those air-filled, high-tech, low-impact shoes those guys wear. Makes me crazy to see joggers putting out all that energy and getting nowhere except back to where they came from. I push this thing around the lawn and when I'm finished I've not only gotten my exercise, my lawn's mowed. These guys will actually *hire* someone to do their lawn so they can jog."

He was oiling the ancient mower when I dropped in. I was trying to write about inflation, I told him. "I have all the facts and figures, but facts and figures aren't necessarily convincing. I mean, I can tell someone the difference between 5 and 8 percent over 20 years is the price of a new *Buick,* that really gets their attention. Because then it isn't just losing 3 percentage points if they don't make the right investment, it's somebody stealing their *Buick.* Understand what I mean, Hoskins?"

"Slow down. You talk too fast." He went on oiling his mower.

"Inflation, Hoskins. How do you tell someone about inflation so that they believe it? I mean, they hear in the news every day that inflation is 3 percent or 5 percent and they just don't realize the impact on their financial planning."

"Just try and remember," said Hoskins, "back to when you were a kid. I mean, even more of a kid than you are now."

"Okay."

"How much did a book of matches cost?"

"Penny matches?"

"Yeah."

"They cost a penny."

"Well now they cost two cents. That's inflation. Happy?"

"Hmmm."

"What did a chocolate bar cost when you were a kid?"

"Quarter."

"What's it cost now?"

"A Dollar."

"Newspaper?"

"Quarter. Costs a buck now."

Hoskins gave the mower a tentative push. It made a lovely, quiet, mechanical, whirring sound. "And that's the same newspaper that tells you how bad the government is for letting inflation get away from us. And the same newspaper that tells us how naughty oil companies are for raising their prices. Know how much a newspaper used to cost at the beginning of the century?"

"I wasn't there, Hoskins."

"Neither was I. But the price was two cents. Two cents in 1900. A dollar today. That's inflation."

"Yeah. Right. Good stuff, Hoskins."

"Hmmm," he said eloquently. "When I was born in 1925, my great-uncle gave me a dollar. That's a bigger deal than it sounds. Guys in car factories were making five bucks a day. Today, to buy the same amount of stuff as I could have bought in 1925 with that single dollar, I'd need over twenty bucks. And that's inflation, too."

He looked at the mower like a farmer looking at a horse somebody's trying to get him to buy. "This machine is a masterpiece. It doesn't make noise. It has no fumes. It doesn't use electricity. It starts every time. It gives you your exercise. What we ought to do, Wharram, is start selling these as environmentally responsible aerobic exercise machines. We'd make a million bucks."

"Yeah?"

"Of course, a million bucks may not be enough. Depends on inflation. Say you had a million now and hid it under your bed. If inflation over the next 25 years equals what it's been over the *past* 25 years, all you'd end up with at the end of those 25 years is about $180,000 worth of buying power when you lifted the mattress and took it out. Even if you never spent a dime."

"But it wouldn't be under the bed. I'd be investing the million. It would be earning *interest*."

"Sit down on the grass, son. I have a few things to tell you." I did what I was told: it's no use doing anything else around Hoskins.

"If you invested your million and got 10 percent interest, what would you earn a year?"

"$100,000. I could live on that."

"Maybe. After taxes, what would the $100,000 be worth? You'd be near the top income bracket."

"About $70,000. I'd be paying about 30 percent in income taxes."

"Now say inflation runs at 4 percent. How much money would you be making a year after 10 years?"

"Hoskins, I don't have my interest tables on me."

"The effect of inflation on that $70,000 would be to make its purchasing power about $30,000 after 10 years. So if you had a million today, invested it at 10 percent, and took out the 10 percent as income every year, in 10 years the purchasing power of your money would be $47,000 after tax."

"So you see, having a million isn't enough. That's what inflation means. Go write *that* in your book."

So I did.

Inflation is the **cancer** of financial planning. As we go through our financial life cycle we can develop good saving habits, we can keep our eyes open for the best interest rates, we can plan our retirement savings, but we still might find that instead of a pot of gold at the end of the rainbow, there's a large lump of soggy porridge.

You have to run awfully hard just to keep pace with inflation. You have to run even harder to beat it. Remember this: if you're in the 30 percent tax bracket and if inflation is 4 percent, you have to get 5.7 percent interest just to keep pace with inflation and the government.

You *can* beat inflation. The following graph is based on figures from the United States, but the experience in Canada is not all that much different.

Check the chart. You'll notice that some investments outperform inflation *slightly*. But after you've paid taxes on these investments, you may actually be falling behind inflation. That's why so many individuals choose to tax shelter their investments in retirement plans.

Other investments put you well ahead of inflation, but as the chart shows, these investments pose fairly high short-term risks. If you're making these investments, you have to be in them for the long haul.

What's Your Personal Situation Now?

The chart on the next page will help bring your own specific situation into a new light. Fill in the blanks. Then take a long, sober look at your retirement plans, your savings, and all the rest of your financial planning.

As the chart shows, investment planning is not as easy as buying a 3–5 percent Guaranteed Investment Certificate and saying it's safe. It's safe in the short term. But over the long term it can actually start *costing* you money because it doesn't maintain the purchasing power of your dollars.

Remember: being a millionaire may not be enough. Not in a country where a book of penny matches now actually costs two cents.

Investment Returns Required to Maintain the Purchasing Power of Investments

(Under various Inflation and Tax Returns)

Inflation Rate (%)

Inflation Rate (%)	2	4	6	8
Tax Bracket	2.0	4.0	6.0	8.0
10	2.2	4.5	6.6	8.9
15	2.4	4.7	7.1	9.4
20	2.5	5.0	7.5	10.0
25	2.7	5.3	8.0	10.7
30	2.9	5.7	8.6	11.4
35	3.1	6.2	9.2	12.3
40	3.3	6.6	10.0	13.3
45	3.6	7.2	10.9	14.5
50	4.0	8.0	12.0	16.0

At my current_____% of tax bracket, and at my _____% projected rate of inflation I will have to earn _____% on a taxable investment just to break even.

The Millionaire's Menu

You've seen the ads. Usually there's a headline that says something like: "How I turned $3.89 into a *million* in seven months—*and how you can, too.*" The rest of the advertisement usually reads like this: "Seven months ago I owed money to three banks. I was on the verge of being thrown out of my apartment. My car was being repossessed. I was down to my last $3.89. *Then* I stumbled across a secret way of making money. It isn't illegal. It isn't immoral. It isn't hard. I only worked two hours a day. *And in just seven months it's made me a million!!* I'm willing to share this secret with you for just $20."

You bet he's willing to share the secret with you. And if he shares it with you and 49,999 other people, he'll have made another million. Working just two hours a day.

One way to become a millionaire is to promise to teach other people how to make a million.

The plain fact is that most of the people who read this book can become millionaires.

Don't believe it? Say you're 30 years old. And say you earn $60,000 a year. If you start "paying yourself first" at a rate of 10 percent, you'll have $6,000 a year to invest. If you put that into a retirement plan annually and got 8 percent, by the time you were 65 you'd have your million. If you and your spouse were both putting in $6,000 a year for an annual total of $12,000, you'd have a $2.4 million to share in 35 years.

Want another way to become a millionaire if you're 40? Buy a $100,000 house. If it gains 10 percent in value every year until you're 65, it'll be worth a million and then some. Two other good things about the investment: you can live in it, with a mortgage of about $700 a month.

Right now, thousands of individual families have "millionaire" status. And there are going to be hundreds of thousands of others joining them in the very near future. Most of them will do it with a *mix* of investments. That mix will not in most cases include very sophisticated investments like options trading or tax shelters. Most of those are for professional investors, and if you read the financial pages you'll see that even the professionals get their fingers burnt.

This book goes over the solid, simple, proven investment alternatives that don't require huge amounts of expertise to buy or huge amounts of time to manage.

There's a chapter on each:

Chapter Six: Retirement Savings Plans. They're the average individual's tax shelter and the easiest way for you to accumulate the money you need to make significant investments.

Chapter Seven and Eight: Real estate. Put 20 percent down and you're making investment gains on 100 percent of the property. That leverage makes it a solid investment and probably the only leveraged investment most individuals participate in. Chapter Eight is about financing that investment through mortgages.

Chapter Nine: Mutual Funds. I believe they're the most satisfactory way for the average investor to participate in the growth of the stock market.

Any of these investment vehicles can be used to elevate you to millionaire status on a kind of "get-rich-slowly" basis. But you have to read *further* in the book. Because along the way you're going to want to take steps to protect your rising wealth.

Chapter 10: Insurance. You're going to need some—but probably not as much as some insurance salespeople will tell you to buy. I've included tips on how to figure out precisely what you need, and how to save substantial amounts by shopping around.

Chapter 11 and Chapter 12: tracking down the ways you're wasting your wealth.

Chapter 13: Divorce—and some other disasters. More than half of all marriages end in divorce and it can hit both partners in the pocket book and the purse. There are ways to soften the blow slightly.

Chapter 14: Retirement—and how to be in the minority of the population that actually gets to enjoy it.

The other chapters? How to get started on your financial "diet" without arguments, without too much pain, and without wasting a lot of time.

All these chapters make up a simple, sane Millionaire's menu. They tell you simply how to make your money, and how to protect it.

Some readers will be irked that I've made it sound too simple. Frankly, once you understand the basics, the general rules are fairly simple. You don't need a computer, a graduate degree in economics, or a shifty tax expert to make a million. You're better off with common sense and some self-discipline.

By the time you finish the book, you'll know that a million is a goal you can reach.

More than that, you'll realize that a million is a goal you'd better reach.

Chapter 4

Welcome to the New Social Order: It's Changed the Way We Plan

In my dad's day, life was all laid out. You went to school. Then you got a job. Then you got married. Then you bought a house. Then you had kids. Then you worked for 35 years. And then you retired, got the gold watch, and started tending the hydrangeas. That was the way things were supposed to work for the middle class, and folks would think you were a little odd if you deviated from it.

I followed the same pattern: education, job, marriage, house, kids. I think this shows a sterling reliability, rock-solid planning, and an enviable maturity. Other people think I'm a predictable bore.

Welcome to the New Social Order.

Today, you can have kids without being married. Or you can get married and choose not to have children. If you are married, there's half a chance you may get divorced and then get married again. The wife may be the primary source of income. The husband may be Mr. Mom. Or the married couple may consist of two men. Or two women. You may never buy a house. You may be a telecommuter and never step inside a downtown office. I know people who take their retirement in chunks: work five years, take one year off. Education doesn't stop at graduation day anymore; it's a continuing process for the executive who wants to survive. People don't have single careers anymore; they have successive careers. They start out as stockbrokers and then transform themselves into holistic beansprout farmers.

All of these changes have had two primary effects.

First, they've made the ads in the personal classifieds much longer. Instead of reading "45-year-old widower lawyer wants to meet respectable lady. Objective: matrimony," you have to wade through: "DWM, ex-police officer, vegetarian, one child, into reflexology, tofu, currently student, needs to meet dominant/equal professional with time left on biological clock. Objective: synergy."

Second, it's made financial planning a little more difficult, and a little more creative. People can't be simply put into slots anymore. It takes a little more investigation on my part—and a little more honesty on their part—to find out in which part of their financial life cycle they are. But, although we're freed of a lot of the constraints that used to affect our parents and grandparents, there are still some eternal verities: we all still have to earn money, have a place to live, and we all still have to plan for emergencies and for when we are unable to work. We may put together the significant events of our lives in a different order than people did 40, or even 20, years ago, but all those events will still happen for most of us.

And it's always better, and cheaper, to plan for these significant events instead of just wandering into them. People who *don't* plan to buy a house end up making lower down payments and paying huge amounts more in interest than people who do plan the event. People who *don't* plan to build their assets don't build their assets. In later years, people who *don't* plan to protect their assets can find themselves with their assets stripped.

Most Individuals Won't Retire

The saddest fact of all is that people who *don't* plan to retire, don't retire. A recent study traced what happened to 100 people from the time they were 25 until they hit 65. At age 65, six of these individuals were still working—whether they wanted to or not. Another 18 were deceased. About half of the people—47—were financially dependent on family, friends, or the government for their living. Which means that 47 people weren't eating steak more than about once a month. Only 27 were financially secure and could enjoy about the same lifestyle they had before they retired. Only two retired wealthy.

Which of these groups do you want to be in? Have you *planned* for it?

You know the point I'm making. No matter how much your life has changed from the one your parents led, you still have to plan for the major stages.

Learning, Earning, and Yearning

When I started as a financial advisor, I used to divide life up into three easy pieces: learning, earning, and yearning.

The "learning" part was pretty straightforward. You learned to be a musician, or an architect, or a social worker. Most of your money came from your family. The financial part of your life was simple.

The "earning" years were more complex. For most people they stretched out for four decades. If you earned an average of $40,000 a year for each year in those four decades, $1,600,000 would go through your hands. If you were married and your spouse made the same amount, $3,200,000 would go through your hands as a couple.

The "yearning" for the most part was retirement. I called it "yearning" because of that recent study I just cited showing only about 29 percent of individuals were achieving what I'd call a dignified retirement.

The others had spent the money, or most of it. They didn't plan. Or if they did plan, they didn't do anything about the plan.

Daniel P. Dwyer wrote an interesting book called The Seven Stages of Financial Planning. In it he defined the process: "Financial Planning is the lifelong process of achieving one's goals appropriate to desired lifestyle by increasing and conserving financial resources, assets and income, both now and in the future."

Sounds simple. After all, planning's easy. We've all planned vacations. And parties. We've planned how to decorate our homes. We plan at work. We help make plans for whatever clubs we're in. Stop for a minute and think over the last few things you planned.

Did you plan them intelligently?

How long did the planning take?

Did the plan work?

Was the planning part of the projects enjoyable?

Usually when I'm talking to people about this, I follow with a question: "Have you spent as much time and effort this year planning your finances?" And just as usually there's some blushing around the room.

People tend *not* to plan their money.

What Colour Car? How Long a Boat?

I asked Hoskins why he figured most people didn't have a plan for their money. He was sitting on a box in his garden, glaring at his tomatoes. They weren't ripening fast enough, and I guess the glare was to let them know he was not happy with their performance. He continued the glare for a few seconds, and then turned to me: "Ever notice that absolutely everyone has an iron-clad plan that details exactly what'll happen when they win the million dollar prize in the lottery? They can tell you exactly what car they'll buy, what trip they'll take, the length of their new boat. Ask 10 people what they'll do with the million and you'll get 10 answers. But you *will* get answers because everybody's secretly planned for it."

He threw the tomatoes a sudden glance to let them know he still had his eye on them.

"But virtually *none* of those same people will have a practical plan for the money they *do* have. And most people these days live in households that are going to earn a million bucks during their lifetimes. They'll plan for the money they have no hope of getting. But they won't plan for the money they've got."

"Yeah ... but *why*?"

"Real money embarrasses people. Sit down with a guy you've never met before in a bar, and in 10 minutes you'll know all about his sex life. But ask your friends how much money they make and they'll change the subject. They're embarrassed because they make too little. Or because they make too much. And because they're embarrassed, they don't want to talk about it—not even to themselves. So they don't plan."

"Yeah ... but *why*?"

He gave the tomatoes another hard look. They weren't going to get away with a thing. He sighed, and it wasn't just about the disloyalty and lack of achievement of his tomatoes. "Maybe, you know, it's one of those great mysteries of life like why men wear neckties and why people put hot water in the ice-cube trays."

A person making $40,000 Can Financially Outperform a Person Making $60,000

Give a person making the average wage a solid financial plan and that person will outperform someone making 50 percent more who doesn't have a plan. Over a lifetime they will get more of what they want. They'll worry less about money and there won't be as many arguments about it.

Chapter 5

Three Tactics, a Lot of Myths

A good personal financial plan rests on three tactics.

1. *Saving money.* If you don't set some money aside then you simply won't have the money you need to carry out the other two tactics. That's why one of the first things this book talked about was *"pay yourself first"*. It *does* take money to make money and paying yourself first gives you the money it takes. Trying to skip that step is like trying to water ski without a boat—impossible.

   Saving money is an attitude it's best to learn when you're young. But if you're forty something or even fifty something you still have time to learn. If you're sixty something and haven't learned the attitude, it's unlikely you'll ever have to. You simply won't have the money to spend. Once you've started saving, you'll find it harder and harder to stop. It becomes a habit; just like spending too much on credit cards is a habit with some. It doesn't make you a skinflint or a miser. It's simply learning not to *need* to spend as much.

2. *Wealth creation.* Just saving money isn't enough. You have to be sure that the money you've saved is working. That's going to require a little work on your part—and some risk taking. Remember, the greater the return, the greater the risk.

   The earlier you start creating wealth, the more wealth you're going to create, simply because your money has longer to work for you: you're earning the interest on the interest on the interest … If you're not so young, the sooner you start the better. But don't take the attitude that "it's too late." Read the charts in this book. You can still magnify your money appreciably.

There's an important point here: the idea isn't for you to create wealth just for the sake of piling up money. That's an idea I find repulsive. Heck, even Hoskins finds it repulsive. The idea is to create wealth so that it'll be there when you need it. Like when you want a house, when you want to retire, when you want to help your children …

3.   *Wealth protection.* Once you've created the wealth, you need to protect it. This usually requires more conservative investments than you used in the wealth creation stage—like bonds, Guaranteed Investment Certificates, and investments in those mutual funds that base *their* strategies on investing in low-risk instruments.

Most people start moving more and more of their accumulated assets into wealth protection type investments as they near retirement. The reason is simple: the older you get, the less you can afford to lose. There's simply not time to try to make it back again.

This book is based on those three tactics. I'm sorry they're so straightforward. Too many people think that dealing with money is somehow magic.

Nah. Ain't magic.

Having a simple investment philosophy is important to wealth creation which is all about growing your capital, protecting your capital and minimizing taxes.

Eighty percent of good money management is so basic ("Why don't you earn it before you spend it?"), so common sense ("Don't forget to pay your credit card off every month") and so down-to-earth ("A penny saved is a penny earned") that people dismiss it. They'd rather believe the kind of tabloid newspaper advice ("Make $1,000,000 investing in Arizona land—*without putting a penny down!!!*"). It's just like 80 percent of really good cooking is so basic ("Use fresh ingredients") that people can't quite believe it, so instead they go for the faddish kind of cooking ("You can make a hit with nouveau blackened Cajun tofu!!!") that results in severe dyspepsia and wilted expectations.

Ain't magic.

Armed with the basics in this book, you'll out-earn the person in the next office who believes that today's investment strategy involves sheltering income in highly leveraged condos and the individual three houses down who *knows*, for sure, that copper is the new gold, forgetting that gold doesn't perform too well these days, and very seldom did.

Ain't magic.

It's probably worth going over some financial myths in order to get rid of them, so we can go ahead, concentrate on the basics, and begin to build your wealth.

Myth: It's how you jigger your income tax.

Reality: You *can* save on tax. But if you're honest, you're not going to make vast gains that will make you rich. And if you're not honest, they'll track you down like a rabid hyena and slug you hard with fines and on-going audits. This isn't an income tax book. There are several fine ones on the market for individuals. Most tax experts will tell you just what I've told you: you can avoid some tax, but you're not going to avoid all of it.

Myth: You just have to hit the stock market at the right time and …

Reality: You don't have time to make it big on the market. Unless you're spending eight hours a day with it, backed by research staff, sophisticated computer programs, and intensive training. And even *they* lose the occasional shirt.

People will walk up to you at parties saying stuff like, "Made a killing on International Crumpet today." Nod politely. Congratulate them heartily. Then wonder why nobody ever walked up to you at a party and said: "Lost my shirt on Multinational Croissants today …"

Winners brag. Losers shut up and have another Scotch.

Myth: Real estate!!!

Reality: This is a dangerous myth because it's partially true. You *can* make money in real estate. Hoskins says *he* has; he's bought several properties that have turned out to be splendid investments.

The problem is that Hoskins bought all of those properties from people who were just trying to learn how to make money in real estate and didn't quite understand the lessons in time. Like the stock market, most people should likely avoid real estate unless they're willing to spend a major amount of time on it.

Myth: Antiques!

Reality: There's money to be made in antiques. And in postage stamps. And in collectibles. And in baseball cards. However, most of that money will be made by antique dealers, postage stamp sales outlets, collectibles vendors, and baseball card touts.

Again a situation where winners brag, and losers shut up and have another Scotch.

Myth: Sheltered real estate investments.

Reality: Some people have made money on sheltered real estate investments, the kind of tax-sheltered property buy that gets you all the magic things: tax relief, leveraged investment, and real estate equity. But, from reading the financial pages and talking to a few investors, it's clear that to make money here you have to:

A) Know tax law;
B) Be solvent enough that you don't have to sell for years in case there's a set back; and
C) Be absolutely, positively sure from hours of investigation that the investment is a good *real estate* investment in addition to having whatever tax perks are promised.

These are definitely not for the amateur. They're not even for most professionals.

Myth: Movie tax shelters.

Reality: Take the "sheltered real estate investments" warning above. Double it. Add some show biz.

If you're anxious to get rid of money, may I suggest the C.N.I.B.? They'll send you a tax-deductible receipt and it'll go towards helping people who can't see rather than going—maybe—towards a movie that'll never be seen.

Myth: "I made $213,000 on soybean futures."

Reality: Don't even think about it unless you're extremely solvent, have super-natural good advisors, and are the seventh son of a seventh son. There's too much downside on the leverage. And that, in plain English, means I'd rather see most people contemplating such an investment take the money to Vegas instead.

Myth: Racehorses.

Reality: Buying them is about as profitable as betting on them, except that there are some tax advantages.

Myth: "Pyramid sales made me a trillionaire in six months."

Reality: The people who make the money are at the top of the pyramid. The people at the bottom are dead. This is the financial version of a chain letter and sometimes only marginally legal.

Myth: Reflated euro-bond time-share oil forwards.

Reality: If you don't understand it, don't buy it. And if the person who's trying to sell you the stuff is the only person you know who claims to understand it, don't buy it. Stick with the brand name stuff that's proven itself. If that occasionally means you skip a chance to buy a Ferrari, it also means you'll pass on the Edsels.

So if all these things are myths, what do you buy to start building your wealth? What the next few chapters suggest are plain-vanilla investments. Nothing exotic, nothing erotic. Boring, but dependable.

Sort of like the person you married—and for the same reason. These are investments you can *live* with. And I believe that if you use these investments within the context of the three basic financial tactics, you'll out perform everybody else on the block.

Unless everybody else on the block has read and *uses* this book.

Chapter 6

Retirement Plans: The Last Investment You'll Need Should Be the First One You Buy

If you can make only one financial goal in life, it should be to make your retirement plan contribution every year. A simple example will tell you why.

Pretend there's a married couple named Bill and Sarah. They're each making $40,000 a year. Each contributes 10 percent of their take-home salary to an Retirement Plan, and continues to do so until age 65. In their tax bracket, their take-home is about $32,000 per year; so their annual Retirement Plan contribution is $3,200 a year each.

Doesn't sound like a big deal, right?

Except when it comes to retirement. After contributing for 40 years—and given an average annual rate of return of 8 percent—they'll each have more than $1,000,000 in their Retirement Plan.

As a couple, they'll actually have about $2,600,000.

That's impressive, but there's more.

Because the government lets you deduct you retirement plan contribution from your taxable income, both Bill and Sarah each get an annual income saving of $640. Which means that as a couple, they have $1,280 *more* to invest every year.

Over 40 years—at the same 8 percent—that $1,280 of annual tax savings would grow to nearly $300,000 if it were invested and returns were made up of deferred capital gains.

Which, when combined with the $2,000,000 within their retirement plan, should put Bill and Sarah among the happier campers, right?

Wrong.

Fred and Wilma are even happier. Both Fred and Wilma made as much as Bill and Sarah. Fred and Wilma contributed just as much and for just the same length of time. But Fred and Wilma decided to *work* at their retirement plan. Instead of settling for the 8 percent annual rate of return that Bill and Sarah got, Fred and Wilma did a little extra research and found a fund that averaged a 10 percent rate of return.

How much difference can two little percentage points make? After 40 years Fred and Wilma had $4,800,000 within their retirement plan—as opposed to Bill and Sarah's $2,600,000. So $2,200,000 is the difference two "little" percentage points made. And if Fred and Wilma had also invested their $1,280 annual tax savings, it would have grown to nearly $1,000,000, assuming investments earned 100% deferred capital gains.

Bill and Sarah's total: $2,600,000.

Fred and Wilma's total: $4,800,000.

Down the road are Harry and Sally. They earn the same as our other two couples. They contribute the same amount. They have the same tax savings. But they really researched their retirement plan, and end up getting an annual rate of return of 12 percent.

Take a guess at what they each have in their RRSP after 40 years.
Harry has $4,448,249.
Sally has $4,448,249.

Together Harry and Sally have $8,896,498. And that's without adding in their tax savings. In fact, Harry and Sally have four times as much as Bill and Sarah—just for earning 4 percent more on their retirement plan.

I think the point I'm making here is very important. The graph on the next page should illustrate very clearly just how important it is. The graph shows what happens to $1,000 over 25 years at interest rates of 8, 10, and 12 percent. The difference that the graph shows is what makes finding a good financial advisor so worthwhile. A good financial advisor can manage your retirement plan that can earn more over time. But there's more to it than that. Because a good financial advisor pays constant attention to what's happening in the economy, he or she can put together a flexible retirement plan that will be able to change to take advantage of a changing economy. That's very necessary. Think about the newspaper headlines over the past three years and you'll see how really necessary it is.

Most people don't do as well as Harry and Sally did with their retirement plan. There are two reasons. First, they don't pay attention to what's happening in their plan. If you go back over the figures, you can see that the difference between Harry and Sally's plan and Bill and Sarah's makes it well worth the difference spending a few hours a month looking at what's happening with your retirement plan.

Let's figure it out. The difference between Bill and Sarah's and Harry and Sally's results was $6,296,498. Over the 40-year life of the plan, that amounts to about $157,000 per year. If Harry and Sally spent five hours a month tending their plan, that would add up to 60 hours a year. For their labors, the couple would make over $2,500 an hour.

Remind yourself of that the next time you push aside your Retirement Plan dossier to watch football instead.

The second reason most people don't do as well as Harry and Sally is that they don't have Harry and Sally's financial advisor. But most good financial advisors could achieve the same sort of solid results that Harry and Sally are getting.

What Happens to the Dollar You Don't Put In

Many people get tempted to skip a year of their retirement planning. Don't.

Every dollar that Harry and Sally put into their plan in the first year turns out to be worth $267 in the last year of the plan. Every dollar they put in during the tenth year of the plan is worth $66 in the end. Every dollar they put in during the plan's twentieth year ends up being worth $16.

Don't skip a year.

In fact, *it's even worthwhile going out and borrowing money to make you plan contribution*. Take out a one-year loan. Pay it back in a year. Because the money you've borrowed will be in your plan and earning money for a lot longer than a single year. If Harry or Sally or Fred or Wilma (I'm sure there's a movie in this somewhere) has to borrow the $2,100 to make their contribution, that loan will cost them under $200 a month to repay.

When you consider the costs of the dollar you don't put in, that's peanuts. When you consider that the interest on the loan they make is only about one quarter of the money they'll make on the tax savings, it's less than peanuts.

Contribute every year—even if you have to take a loan to do it.

Another point: contribute all you can. What happens to the dollar you don't invest tells you why that's true, too. You should make sure your spouse is making the maximum possible contribution as well.

How Do You Buy an Retirement Plan?

I'll tell you how *not* to buy one. Don't wait until one month or two months before the contribution deadline in. Most people do, and if you join them, you'll be lost in the crowd. It'll still be worth making the contribution, but you won't get the kind of cool analysis of your needs that you will at other times of the year.

Besides, the deadline comes too soon after Christmas and too soon before your income tax deadline. Either of those events might tempt you into making less than your maximum contribution. Buy in September. Buy in June. Buy in November. But avoid the rush. Who wants to hurry in a plan that could pay out that much money?

And if you're shifting nervously from foot to foot wondering where you're going to come up with the cash all of a sudden—don't. There's a better idea. There are plans that will allow you to make a regular monthly contribution. Think of them as the regular payments on your retirement. You'll feel the payment in the first month and the second month. Maybe even the third. After that the money will just silently sneak away and continue growing and blossoming for years and years. You don't have to wait until you're 65. And if you haven't started at 40, it's not too late at all. You don't have to wait until you're 65 to start taking money out of your plan. You don't even have to wait until you're 60. In fact, I know people who've cashed in their retirement plan at the age of 45 and used the money for a glorious two-year vacation. It's not a course I'd recommend to the financially prudent, but it can be done. Just remember that you start paying tax on any plan money you take out as you take it out. It's taxed at the same rate you'd be taxed as though the money were income. Take out $20,000 and you're taxed on $20,000 worth of extra income.

Look back at the three couples. If you were Fred or Sarah or Harry you might see how much money you'd put together by the age of 55 and decide it was time to go pick seashells down by the seashore. That's important: a retirement plan can not only give you a retirement that comes equipped with a higher standard of living, but it can also give you a longer retirement.

Would Harry and Sally be satisfied retiring on "just" six million? Maybe. Check the compound interest table at the end of this chapter: how old are they when there's that amount in their Retirement Plan?

Your Retirement Strategies Will Change

All your financial strategies change. When you're younger, it's worthwhile taking a few gentle risks with your investments, trading off those risks against the expectation of higher gains. When you get older, you'll find you become more risk-adverse. You want more conservative investment strategies because you're more interested in protecting money you've already made than in trying to make more. And if you dabble in high-risk investments as you approach retirement, there can be two possible outcomes. You could win big. Or you could lose it all. The downside to high risks for people approaching retirement is just too great to take chances.

Your strategies will also change as the economy changes. A dozen years ago the market was mad about gold. A few years later gold was out and high technology was in. The attractiveness of corporate bonds changes from one five-year period to the next. Sometimes guaranteed investments are the best answer.

You can attempt to watch over all this yourself. You can also attempt to do your own kidney transplant, fix the onboard computer in your car, or play centre for the Detroit Red Wings. In the end, however, the best idea is to find the best financial advisor you can and make him or her part of your planning team.

If you think that's bullroar, think about this: what happened to the last amateur who tried to do your job?

But getting hold of a financial advisor isn't the end of your responsibilities. You have to work with a advisor. When you've got a lot of eggs in one basket, it's always better to keep a close watch on the basket.

I finished writing this and took it over to Hoskins to look it over. He had three things to say about it: "Yep," "Yup," and "Yep." And then he revealed one of his most personal secrets to me. He went over to his beer fridge and reaching way in the back he pulled out two bottles of John Labatt's Special. He took the caps off both and set one in front of me. He tipped some from his bottle down his throat, smiled and said, "There's the odd time in your life when it's rewarding dealing with professionals."

How to Find Your Financial Advisor:

First, let's talk about the importance of finding the professional. This is the person who should have a large positive impact on your financial life. Making sure you have the right planner may mean hundreds of thousands of dollars for you. As with anything that can have an impact of hundreds of thousands, you should shop, and shop carefully.

People in stock brokerages, insurance companies, accounting firms, mutual fund organizations, and banks all call themselves "financial advisor". And there are even some independent financial advisors.

Talk to your friends, relatives, business associates. Tell them all you want financial planning. Then, get three names. Call each of the three and ask for an interview. Ask for an initial presentation to determine your level of comfort level with each advisor.

After the three presentations, fill out the chart on the next page listing the names of the candidates across the top.

There's one other thing you should look for in the planner's proposals. There should be some consistency between all three. If one of the proposals is suggesting something radically different than the others, that could be a reason to raise the caution flag.

And how are you as a client?

Are you clear in your directions?

Concise?

Do you have "stick-to-it-ness" or are you going to be changing your mind every three months?

Do you meet your obligations?

Do you phone your advisor every three months—or just at tax time?

	First Candidate	Second Candidate	Third Candidate
Displayed Competence:			
Displayed Interest:			
Has ___ Years Experience			
Promised Continuing Service			
Talked about more than one type Of Product in Presentation			
Felt Comfortable Personally			
Made Plain How S/He was to be Compensated			
Gave a clear and Concise Program			
Program has liquidity:			
Other Impressions			

Have you given your planner *all* the relevant information?

The better the client, the better the service. The better the service, the better the financial outcome. Be a good client.

Chapter 7

A House Is Not a Home: It's Also a Leveraged Equity Investment

If you made up a list of why you shouldn't buy a house of your own, it would probably look something like this:

"Houses are too expensive right now."

"I don't have enough money."

"Interest rates are too high."

I had the same kind of list beside me on the seat as I turned my four-wheel drive down the road towards Hoskins's house. The list of objections had been written out for me by a young couple who were clients, but I was interested in how Hoskins would look at their points. Besides, it was a Saturday with nothing much to do … and I was thirsty.

He was standing in his garden. He looked at me and then gestured around: "Do you suppose if I planted weeds, I'd get flowers? If I planted Shepherd's Purse, would I get broccoli? If I planted Pig Weed, do you think I'd get prize tomatoes? 'Cause it sure as heck seems to work the other way around." He kicked at an onion top in disgust. "And I suppose you'd like a beer?"

"It's an idea."

I followed him into the house and watched while he rummaged about in his beer fridge. He was taking care to get the proper vintage at the proper temperature. "This is good enough for you," he said, decanting it into a glass and then immediately washing the sediment out of the bottle. Let the sediment dry in the bottom of a bottle of home brew and you'll never wash it out. He handed me the glass and asked for the piece of paper.

"What paper?"

"The one you stuck in your pocket when you got out of your car."

"Ah. Yes. Of course."

Sitting at the kitchen table, he read it and then slammed it down, got up, and headed for his basement. In under a minute—Hoskins is very organized—he was back with a tidy pile of newspapers.

"What they want is a cheap house," he said, ruffling through the paper. "Here we go: three-bedroom backsplit, with in-ground pool, mudroom, country kitchen, family room."

"What price?"

"The asking price is $119,900."

"Where is it?"

"Just around the corner from yours."

I raised my eyebrows: "But I paid ..."

"I know. You paid almost double."

"What's the matter with the place? Bats, rats, termites, nuclear radiation?"

"Nothing wrong with it. The only catch is that $119,900 was the price seven years ago."

"You want me to tell them not to wait until seven years from now." He rose from the table and headed to his beer fridge to get himself a bottle. He always served himself second. I think he thought it made it look as though he were a slower drinker than I was. Pouring the brew into his glass at eye-level, he began talking again: "Each year on my birthday I save the newspaper. There's a big pile going back 25 years. If you take them home and treat them gently you can figure out what's happened to housing prices in this area. You can also look through the classifieds to get a good idea of what people were earning and take a look through the financial pages to see what interest rates were. You could make up some of your little computer charts on them."

Satisfied that his beer was as pristine as possible, he sat on the edge of his kitchen chair and waited for the head to recede. "You know, when Mrs. Hoskins and I bought this house, it was $28,000. I was making $14,000 at the time. She was making children. She yelled. She cried. She said things like '$280 a month in mortgage payments. Plus heat. Plus taxes. Plus maintenance.' At one point I thought I was going to be living in the largest bachelor accommodation in the country. Two years later I was making $16,000, the mortgage payments were the same, and she was still cranky. Then I raised the mortgage payments to pay the place off quicker and she was definitely sulky. Then the mortgage company raised the rates, and she told me she was contacting lawyers about the possibility of having me committed to a comfortable establishment where I would be treated by a large number of male nurses but never allowed to sign another legal agreement. Five years ago we finished the payments and I turned into a financial genius. I couldn't afford the place 20 years ago. Today I really couldn't afford it. My $28,000 house is now worth a third of a million."

He took a slow, self-satisfied sip of his beer and gave a significant little sigh. "And 20 years ago my stupid brother was living in a $190-a-month apartment. He also told me that $280 a month was too much. He's now living in a $1,400-a-month apartment."

"But you've sort of proved my clients' objection that prices are too high."

"They'll go higher. Read the back issues. And the couple will make more money, as I did, and the payments will become easier. Payments on apartments go up every year—even if there is rent control."

"What about the objection that they can't afford it?"

"Did you talk to them at home, Ken?"

"Yes."

"How's their toy inventory?"

"Pretty big toy inventory. The guy's even got one of those apartment-sized wine cellars."

"What would your couple say if you told them that if they worked really hard for five years, skipped the toys, and pulled in their belts, they could end up with $250,000 extra? Tax-free?"

"Come on, Hoskins, real estate prices aren't going up that fast. They're not going to earn that in five years."

"No, but if they make the effort for five years, they'll have the house. Then after 20 years they're going to have the $250,000 tax free. And in the 15 years in between, they'll be paying about what they would have for apartment rent. Or less. If they really want a house they'd have to scrimp. In my day that meant eating a lot of Kraft Dinner. In your clients' case it'll probably mean driving a seven-year-old car instead of a two-year-old one, shorter lunches and—ah—drinking their wine at actual room temperature. That's not much to give up for a quarter-million tax-free."

I looked at my own empty glass pointedly. Hoskins said, "And if you'd started making beer two months ago today you wouldn't be crawling after my beer today."

But he got me the glass anyway. You could tell he was anxious to keep on talking.

"So what about my clients' interest rate objections?"

"Check back in the newspapers. Make your little charts. Generally, you'll find that when interest rates go down, house prices go up."

Even thinking back five years ago, I remembered he was right, more or less. I'd have to do the charts. But charts and graphs and theories don't always work with clients: They have to be *mentally* comfortable with an investment. And that's what I said to Hoskins.

"You're right." He replied. I began to feel a little uneasy. I couldn't remember when Hoskins had told me I was right before. "Let's start by showing them the cost of what *not* buying a house is—year by year." He grabbed a telephone message pad from down the counter and took a stub of pencil from the pocket of his denim shirt. "Let's say, for the sake of argument, that the house they're thinking of is $200,000. And let's also say, for the sake of argument, that house prices in their area go up an average of 10 percent per year. In some areas the average gain over 10 years is a little lower. In some areas it's much higher. But let's keep it simple." He drew up this little chart in his cramped, crabbed handwriting.

Year 1. $200,000.   Gain lost: $0.
Year 2. $220,000.   Gain lost: $20,000.
Year 3. $242,000.   Gain lost: $22,000.
Year 4. $266,200.   Gain lost: $24,200.

Year 5. $292,820.   Gain lost: $26,620.
Year 6. $322,102.   Gain lost: $29,282.
Year 7. $354,312.   Gain lost: $32,210.
Year 8. $389,743.   Gain lost: $35,431.
Year 9. $428,717.   Gain lost: $38,974.
Year 10.$471,588   Gain lost: $42,871.

Total Gain lost through not buying the house over 10 years: $271,588.

I had to hold the piece of paper right up to my eyes to read the tiny writing on it. Hoskins explained: "In year one, if you had not bought the house, you'd have lost nothing. In year two, if you hadn't made the decision to buy the house in year one, you'd have lost $20,000 because the house went up 10 percent while you were dithering. You'd have lost $26,000 in year five alone because you hadn't bought the house five years ago, which would have meant that you would have been making a 10 percent a year gain on year four's value. Got it?"

"Yup. It's simple compound interest. If you don't make the investment, you're not only losing the interest on the investment, but the interest on the interest. If you don't buy the house, you're not just losing the gain on the original investment, you're also losing the gain on the growth of the value of the house."

"Right. Now these figures shake some people up. They look too good. That's another reason I keep those old newspapers around. The houses-for-sale sections show the truth of what I'm saying. Actually, right around where we're living the growth of house prices has been more like 15 percent a year, averaged over 10 years. Some years it's only a single percent. Some years it's been as high as 22 percent. You have to figure out the average for your area." He took his calculations back and peered at them. "But the figures at 10 percent are convincing. If your clients buy this year, they'll pay $200,000. If they wait five years, they'll pay about $292,820. And if they wait 10 years, they'll pay $471,588. And there's another way to look at it. If they buy now and put 15 percent down, they only have to come up with $30,000. Wait five years and put 15 percent down and they'll pay about $44,000 down. In 10 years they'll have to put down over $70,000.

I wondered if this was going to make my clients more mentally comfortable. I must have wondered aloud because Hoskins said: "Tell them to pick the amount of money they feel they can comfortably afford a month. Jot down the figures. Add what they figure they could comfortably save on toys, to what would happen if they kept the car until it was seven years old, to what they'd save if they ate out five times less a month. And then get out your mortgage table and show them how much house they can afford."

That's what I ended up doing. I sat down with my clients and doodled. Their rent was about $850 a month. If they kept their car for a few years longer, they'd save about $250 a month. Cutting back on the eating-out budget would save them about $250 a month. Trimming the toy inventory would save them an easy $200 a month. Total money available for mortgages: $1,750 a month. A $100,000 mortgage could save them about $1,100 a month according to the mortgage table. So they could afford to carry a mortgage of about $150,000 if they spread it out over 20 years. With $50,000 down (which is why God invented parents who will occasionally remortgage their own almost-paid-for-home to provide down payments), they'd have a $200,000 house. They'd have to be very careful with their money for the first five years in order to keep up the taxes and the heat, but …

"I can't see us living in a $200,000 house," she said. "Where would the hot tub go?"

Sometimes I fail my clients. I advise, I discuss, I cajole, I use examples, I phone Hoskins for pointers—but I fail to get them to do what is financially correct. The clients ended up not buying a $200,000 house. Which means, according to Hoskins, they'll have $271,588 less wealth in 10 years.

Hell of a price for a hot tub.

Which House to Buy: A Little Less Castle Can Go a Long Way

Obviously, you want to buy a house that you want to live in. The mental health side of the triangle is important. But the financial side is *just* as important. And because it is, you have to understand a house as an investment, and you should never, ever, take for granted that you're going to make money on *any* house you buy.

Housing markets change across the country. Cities like Winnipeg are fairly stagnant. Toronto is exciting—*too* exciting say some homeowners there. Vancouver and Calgary have their ups and downs. In some single-resource-based towns, housing prices only go down. Canada is not a single homogeneous housing market. The economies of our various regions are different, and so the housing markets are different, just as the weather is different from region to region. That means it's no use watching the national news and trying to draw conclusions about what's happening in your particular area. Because although the national news may be telling you housing prices are up, the homeowners in Lethbridge may be taking a severe beating.

You have to know what's happening in *your* market. And *that* means you have to do a little research. The research is worthwhile because you're looking at an investment that could be taking 20 to 40 percent of your income for the next 20 years. If you sit for a second with a pencil, you can figure out how much money I'm talking about.

Good Research Will Pay You a Lot

The first place to start is your local newspaper. Local papers usually have a big real estate section once a week. Find out when it is and read it every week for a few months. That'll give you a general feeling for where the market is *now*. It'll also get you used to jargon like "VTB," "motivated seller," "carries like rent," and so forth. It will give you a feel for how the game is played, even though you're still a spectator.

One early stop you should make is at your local real estate board. Call them up first and tell them you're interested in getting average and median house prices for the past 10 years. The average house price is just that, but it can be misleading. For example, if nine houses in a town sold for $100,000 and one sold for $1,000,000, the average house price would be $200,000, which doesn't give you and accurate picture at all. The median house price can tell you more. If nine houses sold for $100,000 and one house sold for $1,000,000 the median price would be $100,000 because half the houses sold for $100,000 or less and half sold for $100,000 or more.

Your real estate board probably breaks the figures down somewhat further and may give you figures by particular areas and may give you figures by particular areas and by types of house.

You can also ask the real estate board for figures on the number of units sold per year over the last 10. That'll give you an idea of how often the real estate frenzies hit your area, and whether your area is becoming generally more popular over the years. With this simple research, you're already much better informed then most of the buyers and sellers in your area. And you've begun to do what seasoned and profitable real estate investors do.

Real Estate Goes in Cycles and Trends

Cycles change from year to year, but general trends tend to stay in place over a long period. You can build a chart of average house prices in your area over 10 years and it will show you the general trend, and the specific cycles. And it should tell you whether you're currently in a boom or bust period. Don't simply rely on year-to-year comparisons; go back further and you'll have a much better idea of when to buy.

There's another factor to put into the mix. It's a tool called the "Affordability Index," put out on a regular basis by the Canadian Mortgage and Housing Corporation. It tells you how affordable the average house is for the average home-buying household in your area. It compares average income to average house prices.

In Toronto, a short time ago the Affordability Index crept over 30 percent. That meant that for the average family to afford the average house they'd have to pay more than 30 percent of their income. Most families couldn't face doing that, and Toronto real estate took one of the worst beatings in years.

At the same time, the Affordability index in Calgary was below 25 percent. Most families felt comfortable with that, so houses sold briskly and prices kept rising.

What's the Affordability Index in your area? If it's below 25 percent, there's still room for prices to grow. Mind you, an Affordability Index of 20 percent doesn't guarantee that prices will grow. It may even mean that people are leaving the area and housing prices are going to fall. But in a growing area with an increasing number of house sales and an increasing 10-year price trend, that kind of Affordability Index should be very healthy indeed.

You will not be able to get the Affordability Index figures for the last 10 years; they've only been introduced to the general public lately. But even with the most recent Affordability Index figures in place on your chart, you now know more about the essential health of your local real estate market than most buyers, most sellers, and some of the local real estate agents.

In some cases this chart won't help you. If you want a house right now in Harwood, Ontario, you're going to get a house in Harwood right now and disregard the investment potential. On the other hand, if you're deciding between two suburbs in Calgary, it will definitely help. It would have helped to have had this chart before the last real estate bust in Toronto; the Affordability Index would have signaled the best was possible. It can also tell you when the bust is about to end—if you keep the chart current.

Who's the Real Estate Agent Working For?

Real estate salespeople aren't really salespeople. They're *brokers* and they act for both buyers and sellers. Depending on how you look at it, that could be a comfort ("Isn't it nice they're neutral?") or it could smack of conflict of interest ("How do I know they're telling either the buyer or the seller the whole truth?").

Some real estate brokers are vastly knowledgeable, genuinely kind, and hard working. But one of those vastly knowledgeable, genuinely kind, and hard working real estate broker will confess after a few drinks that there are some amateurs and part-timers in the business.

When you're investing 20 to 30 percent of your income for 20 years, you don't need amateurs or part-timers. On the other hand, just because somebody has been working in the business for 20 years doesn't qualify him or her as an expert. They may simply be someone who has had one year's worth of experience and repeated it 20 times.

Finding a good real estate agent is worth the search. They can save you money. They can save you hassle. They can save you time.

Find five people you know in the area you're buying and ask for a recommendation. Then phone the five agents they referred you to and ask for those referrals. It isn't an imposition. If you were about to spend $10,000 to fix a house, you'd ask for referrals. Doing the same when you're spending $200,000 to buy one makes just as much sense.

Ask the agent where s/he is advertising and then look at the ads. Ask what the agent's specialty is. And then ask to meet the agent at your home.

Lay out two lists of what you want. The first list is what you want for your mental health in a home. The second list is what you want from your home as an investment. Both lists should be prioritized with what's most important at the top, and what you're willing to do without towards the bottom. Your first list could look like this:

- Three bedrooms.
- BIG kitchen.

- Family room separate from living room.
- Workshop.
- Breakfast area.
- Hot tub. (Notice how I put "hot tub" in last as a "gimme"? I'm still mad about that.)

Your second list—"the investment list"—will look something like this:

- Long-term investment: not moving for 10 years.
- $37,500 available as down payment: no more.
- $2,100 available monthly for principle, interest, and taxes: no more.
- Prefer $30,000 down.
- Prefer $1,800 monthly

Make sure that the agent understands that when you say "no more" you mean "not one single bent Armenian pfennig more."

Looking at the House

I can't help you.

I've seen too many bay windows win out over logic and too many big backyards defeat financial planning. I've seen prices go up $10,000 because of two rose bushes.

But I can offer you some gentle advice.

Don't look at it if it isn't in your financial plans. Don't tempt yourself. Refuse to go. Close your eyes. Shut your ears. Lock yourself in the closet. Warn your agent you'll take all these steps if s/he even hints at something out of your range. Or better still, tell the agent you *will* pay extra—out of the broker's commission.

That should clear up the problem.

Don't buy the most expensive house on the block. It'll grow in value more slowly. And the least expensive house on the block can be improved to catch up with the most expensive house.

Before you sign the offer do three things: 1) have your agent show you in writing what other houses in the area have sold for recently; 2) have the house looked at by a professional who can spot future foundation troubles, old wiring, dubious plumbing, slipshod renovations, leaky roofs, and all the rest; 3) get a lawyer to look at the offer.

And, once again, don't pay $10,000 for two rose bushes. Mine got some sort of blight the second year.

Chapter 8

Planning to Burn the Mortgage

It used to be a mortgage was like potatoes. You could have it mashed, you could have it boiled, or you could have it fried—but it was still potatoes.

To understand how times change, you have to understand the basic jargon that mortgage lenders use.

First of all, there's "amortization". That's the length of time it will take you to pay off your mortgage using the rate and payment schedule you select. It used to be that the vast majority of homeowners took mortgages on 20-, or 25- or 30-year terms.

Then there's "term." That's the length of a particular mortgage contract. You may take a mortgage for two years but have a 20-year amortization period.

The shorter your amortization period, the higher your payments. But the less you end up paying in interest in the end. Here's a chart that should make that clear. It's based on a $100,000 mortgage at 7 percent.

Term	Monthly	payment	Total paid	Total interest	Difference in Payment
25	$ 700	$210,123	$110,123	$—	
20	$ 769	$184,635	$ 84,635	$ 69	
15	$ 893	$160,785	$ 60,784	$293	
10	$1,156	$138,713	$ 38,713	$456	

The same compounding of interest that makes a house so worthwhile to buy makes it worthwhile to cut the amortization period as short as possible. Because lending institutions only give relatively short terms of one to five years these days, it's worthwhile *decreasing* your amortization period each time you renew your mortgage. For example, when you first buy the house and you're strapped for cash, you'll get a 25-year term. According to the chart above, that would make your monthly payment $700.

Two years later, after you've gotten a raise, go to a 20-year amortization. That will make your payments $769 a month. Two years after *that* you might be able to go to a 15-month amortization period. That ups your monthly payment to $893, but that kind of total interest savings is worthwhile.

Mortgage lenders are getting smarter and offering more. For example, now many are offering you the opportunity of paying once a week or once every two weeks for your mortgage, instead of once a month. It makes a sizzling difference. You can pay for your house literally years faster, or pay hefty amounts of reduces total interest.

There are more ideas. For example, one firm offers a mortgage that increases your payments on a 25-year amortization period mortgage by 5 percent a year—the amount you'd get in a cost-of-living raise. The effect of raising the payments 5 percent per year means that you pay off the mortgage in 12 ½ years instead of 25.

Want more ideas? Some companies offer you the chance to put in a lump sum on the anniversary date of a mortgage. Whatever the option, the idea is to get the mortgage paid as quickly as possible because that way you reduce the amount of interest payments you ultimately make.

There's a caveat here. Some of these options cost extra money. Don't take the option unless you are reasonably sure you're going to use it.

And shop around. Go to at least three places. Make them talk slowly. Make sure you understand. I didn't the first time and it cost me extra money.

Chapter 9

Mutual Funds, the $3.85 Dollar Bill, and How to Choose a Basket for Your Eggs

Looking at inflation figures always makes me wish I had a time machine. If I could take today's Dollar back to 1970, it would buy me what now costs $3.85.

Unfortunately, time runs in the other direction. What would have cost me just a buck in 1970 cost $3.85 today. What would have cost just one dollar in 1980 would have cost me $1.78 today. What cost me one dollar in 1985 would have cost me $1.24.

Inflation eats away at savings like mice nibbling on cheese, which is why governments say they work so hard at "defeating" inflation by doing things like keeping interest rates high and allowing unemployment figures to swell.

Personally, I've never trusted the government with my finances—I've watched what they've done with their own. So while the government battles inflation in the newspapers, I've chosen another way.

Your savings need to earn at *least* the rate of inflation just to assure that the money you've put away is worth as much as you've put in. In short, the dollar you would have put away in 1970 would have to have earned enough interest to make it worth $3.85 in 2003 just for you to stay even in your ability to buy goods and services. Only if the dollar you put away in 1970 was worth more than $3.85 in 2003 would you have made an actual gain.

If inflation is three percent, you have to be making four to six percent interest in that year to actually stay ahead of the game.

Putting your money in the bank won't put you much ahead of inflation. Neither will putting your money in Savings Bonds. You may squeak out a little ahead, but not much. Check the chart below:

Total Return of Various Investments (1926-1989)
(Arithmetic Mean)

Common stocks	Small Cap Stocks	Long-term government bonds	T-Bills	Inflation
12.4%	17.7%	4.9%	3.7%	3.2%

What the chart says is obvious: putting your money in the bank keeps you *just* ahead of inflation. But if your money performed as well as the stocks, you'd be much better off. In fact you'd be 9.2 percent ahead of inflation.

But investing in the stock market can scare the brass off a bald monkey. People remember the market tumble of October 19, 1987. People have read stories like "The Great Depression of 1990"—which didn't happen. People have heard about how their Uncle Bob lost his wherewithal *and* his shirt when Amalgamated Sundries International slipped down the tubes.

Right.

Look back at the chart. Notice that it *includes* the Great Depression. For most 10-year periods covered by the chart, most stocks grew. And if you were a financial analyst, you'd also know that they grew faster than inflation.

Over the long haul, most stocks grow faster than inflation. *And the right combination of stocks will almost certainly put you well ahead of inflation, even if one of those stocks fails.* With the right combination of stocks your risk is spread, but you still get the inflation-fighting benefits of having your savings in the stock market.

This leaves you with the problem of finding the right combination of stocks. Even with the reassurance from the kinds of charts I've shown you, most people are loath to set out on the adventure on their own. They don't know how to find the right broker, how to read the stock tables, what R.O.E. is, or who Dow Jones is when he's at home.

Which is why *mutual funds* were invented.

Mutual funds are organizations that invest in a wide variety of stocks and bonds, guaranteed investments, money market funds, and even real estate. They spread their risks for safety and yet try to get the largest possible returns. Some mutual funds put more emphasis on safety. Some put more emphasis on returns.

The right way to think about mutual funds is to imagine a large group of investors with a common investment strategy getting together and hiring the best professional investment they can to put that strategy into action.

One group's strategy might be long-term growth of equity—the money they've put into the fund.

Another group's strategy might be regular profits from dividends. They want their money to produce regular payouts.

There are other strategies. There are even "Green" mutual funds, which invest their money only in companies dedicated to improving the environment.

There are funds that specialize in mortgages, in investments in the Far East, in precious metals. But in all cases the essential idea is the same: spread the risk.

There are other things to consider when choosing a mutual fund. The simplest way to decide which fund you'll invest in is to ask the following half dozen questions:

1. Who is the fund manager?
2. How long has the fund manager worked as fund manager for the fund?
3. What is the fund's track record over the last three years?
4. The track record over the last five years?
5. The track record over the last 10 years?
6. Do they have a longer term track record than that?

You have to be aware of who the fund management firm is when you buy a mutual fund. You have to know the costs involved in purchasing the fund. But the key to everything is the fund manager and the fund's track record.

There are several ways to buy mutual funds. You can just buy a lump sum and leave it there. You can put $50 or more a month into a plan. You can buy $2,000 worth every three months. My advice: Do it regularly. Keep building your wealth, bit by bit. Don't skip an investment. *And use a technique called "Dollar Cost Averaging."*

Mr. Wharram's Bedtime Story about Mr. Bull and Mrs. Bear

Dollar Cost Averaging requires that you pay a bit of attention to what's happening with your mutual fund instead of just putting it on automatic and hoping for the best. I recommend the method because it makes your money work harder whether the entire market is trending upward (a "Bull" market) or downward (a "Bear" market). To make the method successful you have to promise yourself to invest a set amount in mutual funds every month.

In my seminars, I usually tell this tale about how Dollar Cost Averaging works. It takes the mystery out of the process.

Mr. Bull buys shares in one fund for five months at $100 a month.

Mrs. Bear purchases shares in another fund over the same five months.

Both of their mutual fund share prices start out at $10 a share. Mr. Bull's shares go straight up over the five months and he cashes out at a splendid unit price if $18 per share, uncorks the champagne, and wakes the next morning with a vicious hangover but still a substantial profit.

Alas, not all fund managers are created equal. Mrs. Bear's fund actually goes down for the first couple of months. Despondency in the Bear household. She sells out at her original purchase price of $10. And then she sets Dollar Cost Averaging into play. And here's what happens after the five months. Take a look at the charts on the next page. Using Dollar Cost Averaging, you can see Mrs. Bear has quietly outperformed Mr. Bull. She did it by keeping to her buying program.

The message is simple: Keep buying. Be constant. Don't fret if your mutual fund is down one day. Or one week. Or one month. If you've chosen carefully—with the help of your financial Advisor—the reasons you bought in the first place are still valid.

The Benefits of
Dollar Cost Averaging

	Mr. Bull	*Mrs. Bear*
	Shares	*Shares*
1st Month	10.00	10.00
2nd Month	8.33	25.00
3rd Month	7.14	50.00
4th Month	6.25	16.66
5th Month	5.56	10.00
Total Shares	37.28	111.60
Final Price/Share	$18.00	$10.00
Total Return	$671.04	$1,116.60
Percentage	34.21%	123.32%

No investment is without risk. Banks have failed, stock markets have crashed. In some years real estate markets have taken astonishing tumbles, and gold isn't nearly as safe as some people believe it is.

Some investments are low risk. These are usually the investments that have a low return: GICs, savings bonds, blue-chip stocks. Investments with higher potential gains also have the potential for higher losses—aggressive common stocks, speculative real estate, peanut futures.

In most mutual funds the relative risk is fairly low compared to the more glamorous investments. But some mutual funds are riskier than others, which is a way of saying that some mutual funds are also potentially more profitable than others.

Choosing how much risk you want to take shouldn't depend on your gambling instinct, or how macho you're feeling that morning. It should have a lot more to do with where you are in your wealth-creation plan, the way an exercise program should be tailored to the kind of physical shape you're in when you are starting out.

If you're starting out—you're fresh, you're feisty, you've got a long way to go before retirement—you can afford some risks. But as you pass 40, you should be taking fewer chances, just as a ball team in a winning position takes fewer chances before the end of the season, and for the same reason; you've got more to lose by taking risks than you have to win. And if the risks don't work out, you're in no position to recover before the season is over.

As you pass 50, you should be taking fewer risks if you're in a healthy position. Minimizing inflation is a risk, and just because you don't have much invested doesn't mean you should be taking a "what do I have to lose?" attitude, because at that stage in the game, even if you have only minor investments, you can't afford to kiss them goodbye.

These things are true of all investments and they're also true of mutual funds—although to a lesser extent, because mutual funds are diversified.

So how do the various types of mutual funds rate on risk/return ratios? Here are some descriptions to give you a better idea.

Higher Risk/Higher Potential Returns

Specialty Mutual Funds

These specialize in particular industries—high technology, oil, precious metals, environmentally connected manufacturers. Usually, the industry is "hot." Often it's like a new musical group—rap, funk/punk/fusion—that has a big intro and then a decline. Mind you, if it does work it works really well. On the other hand, remember the rock group Bionic Bunnies? They're now picking up wet towels in a Gold's Gym in an unfashionable part of L.A.

Balanced Growth Mutual Funds

These invest in a variety of options. Depending on the fund, they may be into money market stuff, and a mixture of shares, bonds, and debentures. The risks and rewards they experience depend on the mix. Some go for more growth; others go for slower growth. There are two ways to judge them. You can do a long, detailed analysis of their investments and how they've mixed them. Or you can look at their track record over at least a five-year period. I'd do the latter. Their "balance" depends on their managers.

Fixed Income Mutual Funds

You've heard of people sitting back and "clipping coupons" for their living. This is what this kind of fund is about. Usually, they blend bonds, debentures, fairly conservative money market instruments, mortgages, and preferred shares. The goal is to give you money month after month rather than growth.

Bond Funds

Just what the name says—they invest in bonds. But not all the bonds are government bonds; some are bonds issued by blue-chip corporations. The reason you invest in this kind of fund is to make money from short- and medium-term bond fluctuations, which means that the fund's management really has to keep an eye out for those fluctuations and be willing to hop on to a different train if a faster one shows up. Also, bonds are competing with the stock market. Generally speaking, when Wall Street's up, bonds look a bit tatty, and vice versa. Obviously, the average investor—and that includes me—is not going to be able to forecast some of these stock-bond market shifts. That means that, as with any other fund, you need solid management.

Equity Funds

Go back and read about bond funds. Bond funds are like giving a company— or a country—a loan. Equity funds are buying shares in their growth and the amount of profit they make every year. Whether the equity fund pays more than the bond fund depends on the year. You need solid management. Have I said that before?

Mortgage Funds

For most Canadian homeowners, "paying the mortgage" is the monthly priority. They'll put down $837 on their house before they'll do it for food, or a computer, or boats, or a car. That makes these funds solid and safe—unless the mortgages that are held by the fund are on marinas or computer warehouses or strip malls. How good—and how conservative—the fund is depends on what the mortgages are. Remember that even the Reichmanns have sometimes had some difficulty renting out space to cover their mortgage costs on office buildings.

Preferred Income Mutual Funds

These are specifically designed for conservative and elderly investors. There's a good income after tax and a dividend tax credit, and a very heavy emphasis on preferred shares that are buffered against most market shocks and fluctuation.

Lower Risk/Lower Potential Returns

I could probably rewrite the list above every year, giving a different place on the risk/reward scale to some of the funds depending on market conditions. Bond funds are really satisfying to be in when the market tumbles. Equity funds are great when there are great increases in the market—or even when you're holding steady year-after-year period of growth. Mortgage funds are great when …

So why did I write all these definitions? Actually they're valuable to look over when you're expecting a mutual fund sales representative to come calling. They give you something to talk about and they let you know that *no* mutual fund is perfect: you're never going to earn a trillion yen in perfect safety here or in any other investment. However, promise me that you'll look over the reasons why I've been so insistent about getting involved with mutual funds in the next section. And be aware that most of *my* investments are in mutual funds.

But always check the fund manager. Check their long-term record.

Why Are You Buying Mutual Funds?

1. *Because you can sell them fast.*
Rules on selling your mutual investment vary from fund to fund. Check the fine print. But most of them are given a *value* every day, and the law says they have to give you that money within seven days. That's faster than you can liquidate a house or Great Aunt Emma's ruby bracelet. Check, however, for penalties.

The fact that mutual funds are liquid and are valued may be of considerable advantage in estate planning. If you die and leave a house, it may be months before you sell and your heirs get all the advantages they should.

2. *Because you can get tax breaks.*
Dividend income and capital gains from mutual funds—as with some other kinds of investments—are handled differently than regular income you get working nine-to-five. In most cases, capital gains are the most tax-efficient form of income to earn since only 50 percent is taxable, followed by dividends and then interest income. Because they're a moving target, you'd best consult your accountant or financial advisor.

3. *Because it's a crowded market: people are competing for your investment.*
Last time I counted, there were thousands of mutual funds. They compete for your investment. But there's an added advantage. Mutual funds are required to make full disclosures. They have to tell how they've done in the past. How they charge you to make their profit. What their policies are. Comparing two- or twenty-mutual funds is easier than comparing two cars. All you have to do is remember to ask the right questions ("Who manages the fund, what is the track record?")

and follow the other rules in this chapter and you'll be a much better than average consumer of mutual funds.

4. *Because most mutual funds are flexible.*
Most offer more than one kind of fund. They have a hotshot fund for when you're starting out, a growth fund for when you want to do some middle-age-spreading of your investments, and some income protection funds for when you don't want to fret anymore. With most, you can shift from fund to fund without the kind of charges it costs you to buy into the fund in the first place. Check. Double check. Funds also offer to reinvest your dividends, interest, and accrued capital gains. Check their procedures.

5. *Because they offer different ways to purchase.*
You can buy with simple monthly payments. You can buy with cash. You may get an advantage with a group investment plan set up within your company. Don't judge one plan on its own. Check it against another—and then another. The exercise will bring you more of an understanding of how things work—and of how you really want to do things.

6. *Because you can use a mutual fund to secure a loan.*
You can even use the mutual fund you're about to buy to secure a loan from your bank to buy the mutual fund you're about to buy. Reading that back to myself, I realize I've made it difficult to understand. Let's make it simple. You can go to the bank. You can tell them you want to buy $500 or $5,000 worth of mutual funds and ask them to lend you, say, $250 or $2,500 to do so. The rest of the money you put up yourself. The reason you'd do this is that you hope that the mutual fund pays you more than the loan costs. This is leveraged investing—the kind of investing you do when you buy a house with $25,000 down and hope that the real estate value goes up faster than mortgage interest payments.

Maybe it works. Maybe it doesn't.

I'd like to ask at least three people other than the person selling the mutual fund what they think of the idea in your particular case. I'd chase the figures around the kitchen table for a couple of nights.

For some people leverage is absolutely the right idea. For others it's putting themselves on ground so shaky it's going to make them seasick. Remember, you must have good cash flow and time for leverage to work. But the most important thing to remember is that you must feel comfortable with the concept.

However, aside from using a mutual find as collateral to buy itself, you can also use it for collateral to buy a house or a car. What the mutual fund gains may pay for the interest on a loan. On the other hand, for things like cars, stereos, boats, and vacations, it's better to save the cash first and avoid using your long-term savings for toys.

What Kind of People Invest in Mutual Funds?

Some of the proof of how good an investment is, is the kind of people who are making the investment. Surveys show that mutual fund buyers are better educated than average, pay more attention to their investments than other kinds of investors, and earn more from their jobs than people who pump their money directly into the stock market. It's also a myth to think that direct stock market investors are wealthier than mutual fund investors: most mutual fund investors have bigger portfolios.

In short, if you invest in mutual funds you're in well-educated, high earning, and fairly well off company.

Chapter 10

The Insurance Man Only Knocks
About Eighteen Times

Hoskins laughed. "We used to call him the 'wiper'. If you hear the doorbell and open your front door to find a man wiping his feet, *of course* you're going to invite him in. Why would he be wiping his feet if he *wasn't* going to come in?"

"The wiper" was an old-fashioned life insurance salesman, the kind that read marriage notices so he could turn up—wiping his feet—on your doorstep to sell you a policy to take care of your increased responsibilities. The wiper read birth notices and sold policies that would not only ensure the child's life, but make sure the child got through college. He watched for corporate appointment notices so that he could sell further insurance because of the higher level of income people would have to replace.

"I used to actually invite insurance salesmen to the house just to see how hard they sold," Hoskins said. "Being in marketing myself, it taught me a lot. How to use your client's emotions. How to sell the future. All that stuff." Hoskins himself was actually the manager of a company that sold heavy equipment: 'dozers, backhoes, graders. But the principles were still the same. "And I used to tell my salesmen to do the same things: if you want to know how to sell, invite an insurance agent over to the house. Watch him sell something that you can only cash in on after you're dead."

Insurance salespeople have improved, but they're *still* good salespeople and they *still* get higher commissions for insurance products that may not be suitable for you.

There's a right way to buy insurance. And a right person to buy it from.

Taking the time to buy insurance the right way and find the right person is a short job that could save you thousands over the years.

Wharram's Basic Principle: Insure Against the Worst First

What's the worst thing that could happen to your family? Your death? Your house burning down? Your spouse's death? A permanent disability that leaves one of you unable to work? *Insure against the biggest catastrophe first.*

If you're a fairly young family, it is likely that the worst thing that could happen would be the death or disability of one of the wage earners. Figure it out: how much income would you have to replace and for how long? And how much *added* income would you require if one of you died? You may need extra income for childcare, for example.

Sit down with your spouse for an hour and write down the answer to that simple question: If one of you died, how much income would have to be replaced for how long? And how much insurance coverage does it take to replace that income?

If you figure that you'd need about $50,000 a year for five years, your total insurance need is—roughly—$500,000. Remember you have to factor in inflation. If you'd need the equivalent of $50,000 a year for 20 years, you would also have to factor in inflation to generate the income that will preserve your money's buying power.

The income you need may actually decline. Perhaps you'll have paid off the mortgage in three years. Perhaps you'll have cut the cords and seen your children exit into the work force in five years. If those things are the case, maybe you need several policies. One to cover your mortgage. Another to last until the kids are on their own. And then continuing policies that will let your spouse continue to have an income.

Figure it out. Then figure out the answer to another question: *"How much money would it take to replace one of your incomes if one of you were to become permanently disabled?"* You may need more money in the event of disability than in the event of death. Because in the event of disability you may have extra medical expenses, and you certainly do go on eating, wearing clothes, and needing entertainment. And over the next 10 years most of us are far more likely to become disabled than to die.

Could your family survive if one of the wage earners were disabled for two years? Or five years? *What monthly income would you need to replace that wage earner's earnings?*

There's one other basic insurance need for most people: liability insurance. Being sued for $1,000,000 because your boat, or snowmobile, or car killed or injured someone, or because some door-to-door insurance salesman slipped on the ice you'd forgotten to clear off your front steps can be quite catastrophic. It could lock up your income for life. Getting liability insurance against these things is relatively cheap. Raising your liability insurance on your car from $1,000,000 to $2,000,000 may cost under $20 a year, but could save you from dozens of years of toil if you were sued for one of those handsome figures you read about in newspaper headlines.

There's other insurance, too. But the point is to *insure against the worst first.* I've inserted a chart that'll help you work out what you need. The chart is valuable for two reasons. First, because it really brings home how much insurance you need. Second, it's a protection against over-buying.

	How much?	*How long?*
My death	_____	_____
Your death	_____	_____
My disability	_____	_____
Your disability	_____	_____
To pay house	_____	_____
	How much?	*How long?*
To raise kids	_____	_____
To pay off other major investment	_____	_____
	We own the Following	*We have liability on*
House	_____	_____
Car	_____	_____
Boat	_____	_____
Snowmobile	_____	_____
Other	_____	_____

Hoskin's Basic Principle: Insurance is Insurance and It Ain't Nothing Else

You can buy life insurance that also has a savings plan built in. You can buy insurance that allows you what looks like cheap loans. You can buy life insurance that also promises you early retirement.

Don't.

"It's sort of like buying a lawnmower that the guy also promises can do your laundry. When something's doing two jobs, it isn't doing either one as well as it could. Either you end up with your clothes mowed or your lawn dirty."

Hoskins is sometimes difficult to understand, and I told him so. He pulled the lever on the side of his La-Z-Boy, leaned back, stared at the ceiling, and started to explain. "Okay. The insurance man promises you life insurance. And he tells you it's also a savings plan, or a pension plan. That's when you start reading the fine print. If it *is* a savings plan, it's twisted. Because the insurance company—check the fine print—is actually charging you money to put money into the savings plan. No bank does that. And when you want to take your savings you lose your insurance policy. And if you want to borrow money from your savings plan, you'll be charged interest to borrow your own money in most cases. Insurance is insurance and it ain't nothing else."

And insurance that is just insurance—like term insurance—is a lot cheaper than insurance that also tries to do something else. If you buy plain-vanilla insurance with no additives, bells, or whistles, you'll buy a lot cheaper.

Or you'll be able to buy a lot more insurance for the same money. Because plain-vanilla term insurance can cost you one-half to one-third of what whole life or Universal Life insurance will cost. Skipping the savings plan will leave you enough left over to start your own savings plan. And if you work at it the way this book tells you to work at it, you'll likely end up with a better-performing savings plan and a bigger endowment.

Remember that most insurance companies pay sales-people higher commissions to sell the lawn-mowers-also-do-laundry policies. Which may explain why those salespeople are pushing the idea so hard.

Wharram's Other Basic Principle: Get the Right Insurance Person

My view is that insurance people shouldn't come looking for you—*you* should go looking for insurance people. That lets you be picky, and picky is what you want to be. Between your car, your life, your house, and your disability insurance, you're going to be paying impressive sums over the years. You're a package that some insurance representative will find very worthwhile even if you're buying your insurance at the lowest possible rate for the coverage provided.

Go to the smartest person you know. Ask who she deals with.

Go to the richest person you know. Ask who he deals with.

Go to your financial advisor, *if* that person's *not* connected with an insurance company. Ask who she deals with.

You'll find they shop around. That's important. One company can sell you $100,000 worth of term insurance for less than another. And you want to be able to choose.

Talk to the agent. Consider his/her attitude. And then hand over the chart you've prepared on your insurance needs. The agent should say something like: "I'll have to get *quotes* on the life and the disability insurance." You should expect quotes from at least two and possibly three companies. After all, your insurance is going to cost you more over your lifetime than a car would, and you wouldn't pop in and buy the first car you saw.

Over your lifetime you're going to make more than one visit to your agent. You're going to want more insurance when you buy a house. When you buy a car. When you get the big new job. In fact, you'll need more insurance on all those cases where "the wiper" used to come calling at your door. But *you* should be in control. *You* should know exactly what you want—and for how long. And you should stick to your guns.

"And if the guy with the fancy products from the life insurance keeps calling you on the phone, just explain that you're on the way to the doctor to get a CAT scan for acute Dysan syndrome," said Hoskins.

"What's acute whatever syndrome?" I asked.

"I don't quite know myself. Except that it scares the hell out of life insurance salespeople."

Chapter 11

The True Cost of Toys

As I was writing this, I remembered last Christmas.

I was just down the hall from where the Christmas tree was. It was a very nice plump tree, decorated with a lot of care by my wife. There was clattering in the kitchen and children on various phones telling various friends what they had received and comparing that with what their friends had received. There were an awful lot of "yeah, well *I* got's" being said on our end of the line. I'd been smiling as I listened in, and then I caught myself looking across the fence at a neighbour's new car.

Two years newer than ours.

Probably has a GPS.

Four-wheel drive.

Cellular *fax*.

I felt a little resentment. In fact I felt a lot like my kids on the phone: I wanted to phone him up and say, "Yeah, well *I* got ..."

There's a place down in Los Angeles—where else?—called "The Toy Shop." It sells cars—Ferraris, Lambos—basically anything that's very red, very expensive, and very fast. The name of the place is playful yet accurate. As the lady down the street says, "The only thing that changes with the size of the boys is the size of their toys."

I thought she'd been talking about something else until I detected my envy for the neighbour's new car. After that I took a walk around the house and listed the toys: the men's toys, the women's toys, and the family toys.

You might want to take a piece of paper and go through the whole embarrassing exercise the way I did. You list the toy. You list what you paid for it. You list when you bought it. You list how many times you've used it. You make a note of the last time you used it. I've put a sample form at the end of this chapter.

Make 10 photocopies of the results. You wrap one copy around each of your major credit cards (And don't think I'm kidding about this. The idea is as effective as putting a full-length mirror on the fridge door when you're dieting.) The idea is that the next time you see something you must absolutely have, and right now, you reach for your cards, and you find that you don't even have to unfold the toy inventory you did. Suddenly, you're just not in a buying mood.

I phoned my friend Hoskins, the free-spending miser. "Whatcha get for Christmas?" I asked.

"HDVD player," he said. "Cost Emily $289, but it's got a lot of features."

I hung up. I hang up on Hoskins a lot. I looked at my toy list. I bought a VHS about 20 years ago. It cost about $1200 in those days. I was the second person on the block to get one. We don't use it. It plays only Beta format and Sony lost that argument to the VHS supporters. Two years after getting it, we bought a VHS format machine. It had more features than the old one, played the tapes that the video shops actually rent without snickering at you, and it cost under $800.

And Hoskins is sitting around watching a machine that's better than mine and cost less than half *that*.

Remember the first digital watches? Cost $500, and if you had a flashlight you could tell what time they claimed it was. These days you can buy them for four dollars at the milk store and they'll also dice carrots, take you're pulse, and keep your golf score. And remember the first pocket calculators? Then, $600. Now they come in cereal boxes. The one I use now costs $10. It's solar-powered. It will outlive me. It deserves to. It's smarter than I am.

Over the past year I talked to a lot of people, myself included, about the true cost of toys. I kept taking out my list and fooling with my calculator. I got other people to make lists and fool with their calculators. Occasionally, I'd phone Hoskins and hang up on him.

The result: In the past year I have *not* spent $1,000 on toys. The calculations:

If I saved the $1,000 that I would have spent on toys and invested it at 8 percent, and if I'd done that for the last 10 years, I'd have $14,486 in the bank today.

If I'd done the same thing for 15 years and invested at 8 percent, I'd have $27,152.

20 years, $45,762.

30 years, $113,283.

All those calculations are at 8 percent. I pointed the calculator at the sun and figured out what I'd have if I were earning 10 percent on that $1,000 a year.

> After 10 years, $15,937.
>
> After 15 years, $31,772.
>
> After 20 years, $57,275.
>
> After 30 years, $148,557.

In short, at 10 percent, if I worked 30 years and saved just $1,000 a year on toys I wasn't going to use much, I'd have $164,494.

Fine.

But I watch my investments, so I get 11 percent. Here's what would happen to the same $1,000 a year:

After 10 years, $16,722.

After 15 years, $34,405.

After 20 years, $64,203.

After 30 years, $182,299.

A lot to *pay* for toys—$199,020. And we're not even talking about recreational vehicles, or 31-foot sailboats, or motorcycles here. All we're talking about is $1,000 a year.

It gets worse- or better-depending on how you look at it. Guess what the figure would be if you saved $1,000 on toys and received 15 percent on your investment over the 40 years most people work in their lives?

Come on. I dare you.

The answer is $1,676,647.

There are probably a lot of you out there saying, "Yeahbut, yeahbut, yeahbut ..." it's the "*yeahbuts*" that get us every time. Let's deal with them.

"Yeahbut, I don't spend $1,000 on toys a year."

Check your list. I'd bet you do. Did you count the year you got the CD player and the leather interior when you bought the new car? *That* cost you $1,000 or more. What about the time you spent the $ _____ on the boat or snowmobile or whatever? Could you have shaved a grand off the price and taken your toy budget down?

Which toys do you have that could have waited a year—and would have cost you less? Remember my DVD/VCR story?

And you may buy several small $200 toys a year. Check your closet. Look in the garage. Behind the furnace. Check the kitchen. When was the last time you used the food processor or the automatic digital microform three-way whatever? Matter of fact, when was the last time you used the automatic clock on the stove?

Then check out the $100 toys. And the $50 toys. Add them up. I did and I'm too embarrassed to tell you the answer.

And my kids keep muttering, "$1,676,647" and asking if we could sell the radial-arm saw, the video cassette player and the cappuccino machine.

"Yeahbut, I only have 10 years before I quit."

Yeahbut, don't you want to be richer when you quit? Check back on the figures. If you're 50 now and quit in 10 years, what could you buy for that $15,937 or $14,486 or $16,722 that you'd really need and want then?

In 10 years you could retire with all new toys.

There's another thing. Just because *you* quit working in 10 years doesn't mean that your money has to quit working. It can go on compounding and compounding until you need it or want it. That may be in 20 years instead of 10. Go back and check the 20-year figures. Or the 15-year figures.

"Yeahbut, I really like my toys."

Check your list again. Think back. And think hard. How long did you *really* like them for? If you think about it this way, you may decide you may as well have rented the darned things. How much did the boat cost you per-day-used last year? The Cuisinart?

"Yeahbut, you gotta live now!!"

And you're going to have to live 10 or 20 years from now. How many toys will you have thrown away by then? How many toys will you be able to afford?

The reason I know all these arguments is that I had them all with myself.

It gets *even* worse. The toys go on the credit card. And if they stay on the credit card, you're paying—at this writing—17 percent per year and more. You get one toy paid off and the next one goes on.

Seventeen percent per year going to the bank—instead of 8 percent per year coming from investments. That's a 25 percent difference. You can say, "yeahbut"; however, it's close enough to being true. Net loss: $250 a year. If you *had* that $250 a year, you could add over a third to the toy money you were tucking away. And if you did add that you'd end up with …

You figure it out.

After 40 years and at 8 percent you'd have about $65,000 extra. That's $1,741,647 instead of that measly $1,676,647. And there's another good reason to keep a toy inventory wrapped around each credit card. Or to hide the credit card behind the spice rack. Or not to apply for the thing in the first place. Remember Wharram's Credit Card Ruling: "One credit card, kept up to date."

Developing an Attitude About Toys

I went down to Hoskins's place and asked him about his toys. I showed him my calculations. I showed him my toy inventory. I bared my soul. I bared the souls of people I'd talked to about toys. Hoskins nodded and said, "Yup."

I didn't hit him.

Then he said, "Put it off for a year. If you see a toy and want a toy, put it off for a year."

I must have looked puzzled, because he continued.

"If you put it off for a year, it actually gets a number of bonuses. I was looking at a camera two years ago. It had single-lens reflex, through-the-lens metering, zoom lens, motor drive. Cost maybe $550, which is not too expensive if you're into those things. Nice toy. I put it off for a year. In the meantime, I read some camera magazines. I got to know a lot more about what I was buying, which made me a smarter consumer. The magazines let me know exactly what I should be buying, and exactly how I would use it when I did buy it. After a few months of reading magazines, I realized I didn't need as much camera as I had been going to buy. I wouldn't need the motor drive for one thing. And if you know what you're doing, that through-the-lens metering stuff can actually hold you back from the kinds of pictures you really want. So at the end of a year when I did go back to the store for a camera, I was able to save money. What I needed cost me only $280, instead of $550. That was partially because I was buying less camera and partially because prices had come down. So that gave me $550 to invest for a year while I was making up my mind. And it saved me $270. It made me richer. And it made me smarter." He played with his coffee a bit. "But the main thing about waiting for a year and reading up on it is that you often find you don't want the toy after all. The passion fades. Which also makes you richer." He took the last sip from his coffee. "One of the articles I read in the magazines said that at one point the Polaroid people were selling more cameras than they were packages of replacement film. People would buy a camera, run through one package of film and then put the thing in a closet. The passion fades." He looked at me. "How many cameras do you have in your closets?" He kept watching as I went through the mental exercise.

"About three or four," I said.

"That's the other good thing about waiting a year for your toys. Saves you a lot of money on closets, too."

He walked over to the stove and shook the coffeepot to see if there was enough for another cup. There wasn't. "There's one last thing about toys. If you cut down on the number of toys you get, you're going to get better with the toys you *have*. Whenever I get the itch for a new toy, I have a secret ceremony. I haul myself out to the store, go home, and go to the basement and make a make a batch of beer. I've become pretty good at it; my stuff's as good as some of those microbreweries. I put up four dozen bottles of bock about three months ago when I was itching to buy one of those giant television sets. Should be ready now. Want to try a bottle?"

I nodded.

"Good. Then I'll have one myself and we can watch the game. I find that if you sit about three feet closed to the screen you get the same effect as one of those giant models."

He was right about the beer.

And about the television. Three feet closer and it looks as big as the giant ones.

You could really come to hate the man.

The Attitude Adjusters

1. Take the toy inventory. If you're like me, it'll prove to you that you're spending money on toys that you just don't use. Keep a copy of the toy inventory with your credit cards.
2. If you're considering a really big toy—a boat, a recreational vehicle, a horse—rent one for the first few times. And stick around while the person who's renting it to you is getting it ready to go or putting it away after you're done.
3. Wait a year. Heck, even if you wait just six months, you could get the things at an off-season sale price.
4. Before you get the toy, get a magazine or book that tells you about the toy. Hunt down some people who know something about the toy in question. Ask them about its good points and its bad points. You'll end up smarter about the toy if you finally do decide to buy.
5. Get good at one thing and stick to it.

6. Remember the triangle. Sure a toy is going to bolster up the mental side now but it's taking away from the financial side, which means you could be in trouble later.

The Toy Inventory

Toy	Cost	How often used	Last used
1. HDTV	_____	_____	_____
2. Boat	_____	_____	_____
3. Computer	_____	_____	_____
4. Rowing machine	_____	_____	_____
5.	_____	_____	_____
6.	_____	_____	_____
7.	_____	_____	_____
8.	_____	_____	_____
9.	_____	_____	_____
10.	_____	_____	_____
11.	_____	_____	_____
12.	_____	_____	_____
13.	_____	_____	_____
14.	_____	_____	_____
15.	_____	_____	_____
16.	_____	_____	_____
17.	_____	_____	_____
18.	_____	_____	_____
19.	_____	_____	_____
20.	_____	_____	_____

You may need more space than this. I did. I took my inventory by walking through every room in the house, poking through closets, pacing around the garage, and ferreting through the basements.

Chapter 12

The Chapter That Dares Not Speak Its Name

Most financial books leave out a lot. They'll tell you about an "advanced bear phase approaching termination" with all the excitement (and detail) of Aunt Roberta showing you her pictures of her trip to the Grand Canyon, but they don't tell you much about divorce. They'll relate with relish the anatomy of a "no-load front-end option" or "inter-vivos trusts" and how those things can make you lots of money, but they forget to tell you how to get the money for the investment in the first place. This is understandable. Things like divorce and saving are depressing topics.

So's this one. It's about cars.

People love cars. There are enough cars in North America to go around the world almost three times if they were parked bumper-to-bumper—a situation the country seems to get into on most summer long weekends. More than 25 percent of the land area of most cities is covered with roads or parking lots. There are car magazines, car television shows, car exhibitions, car songs, car contests, important parts of radio programming given over to telling you just where all the other cars are headed. We love our cars.

We should. They cost us enough.

For most people, a car is the second biggest investment they'll ever make. And that's *despite* the fact that everybody knows the moment you drive off a dealer's lot, you've already taken a big shot in the wallet.

Let's say the average car lasts 10 years. That means it's losing about seven percent of its value every year on a compounded basis. The losses are stiffer in the early years, but they continue until the vehicle's ready for the scrap yard.

But the *initial* cost of a car is only part of what you're paying. The *real* price is going to astound you; it does most people I tell it to.

Take the cost per kilometres you'll drive. Multiply it by the number of kilometres you'll drive this year. *That* gives you part of the cost of driving.

There's more.

Add insurance.

Add license and registration.

Add parking.

Add tickets.

Then add the cost of your car payments.

Then, because the value of your investment is going down, add depreciation. For simplicity's sake, take seven percent of your car's cost when you bought it—and think of it as an annual charge. Depreciation varies a lot from car to car and even from area to area, but seven percent will give you a general idea. Here, I'll give you some space to write this all down.

Operating cost:
_____kilometres X cost per km   = $_____
Insurance per year: = $_____
License and registration: = $_____
Parking: = $_____
Tickets: = $_____
Payments: = $_____
Depreciation: = $_____

Go back to the interest table in chapter six. How much accumulated wealth would you have if you invested that money instead of putting it into a car?

I can hear you now. You're gnashing your teeth. You're saying stuff like, "I *need* my car."

I warned you this wouldn't be a very easy chapter.

You Don't Have to Give Up a Car

There.

Happier?

A lot of people *do* need their cars. But take a second and finish the following sentence: "I need my car to _____."

Most people will finish the sentence by adding something like "to get from Point A to Point B." The plain fact is that you can get from A to B in a new car that costs under $10,000, gets x number of kilometres to the litre, depreciates less, costs less to finance, and costs less for maintenance than most of what you see beside you on the freeway. That's one way to save money.

Or you can keep your car longer. Anytime you feel the need to go and buy a new- or newer-vehicle, take five minutes. Figure out the additional financing charges. Figure out the additional financing charges. Figure out the additional depreciation. Consider the fact that older cars cost less to insure and call your agent to find out what your new insurance rate would be on the car you're thinking about and what your savings would be by keeping your present vehicle. Then turn again to the interest table in chapter six. Figure out how much total wealth you'll be spending by not keeping the older vehicle.

Or, if you can't stop yourself from buying *one* car, you can probably stop yourself from buying *two*. A large percentage of families now have two cars. But do they really need them—especially when the cost of owning and running them is so high? Can you make do with just one? Keep a diary of all your combined trips. Which ones absolutely demand a second car? Which ones could have been put off until later? Which ones could you have used transit for instead? Which ones would have been a 15-minute walk? Which ones could you have done with a healthy you-need-the-exercise-anyway 10-minute bike-ride? Which ones could have been done by car-pool? Which ones could have been done with a rented car? Keep that diary for a month. After all, the chore of doing the diary for four weeks is worthwhile if it can save you the kind of money we're talking about here.

Another way to save money is to use your car *half* the time. You'll spend half the amount of money you do now on those "per kilometre" charges for oil, gas, tires, and maintenance. And, according to the Automobile Association, you'll cut out about 25 percent of your depreciation costs.

There are other points to ponder. By driving less, you pollute less. That's one of the reasons governments have ordered car companies to improve the average fuel economy. If we all drove less, streets would be less crowded, and so would parking lots, and we'd free up valuable urban land for housing. People would be healthier. Transit systems could afford more vehicles because there'd be more demand, which would mean that transit would get easier to take. And …

You still love your car.

I understand. I've stood beside a 22-year-old in a car showroom and patiently explained that he could have the cherry red rag top rocket he was looking at *or* put the money into his Retirement Plan instead and have over $300,000 waiting for him when he was 65.

Guess what his decision was?

Right.

We're going to go on being smitten by our cars. The point here is to understand what the true cost of our love affair is and not kid ourselves about it. If we stop looking at the Hyper Tri-turbo with the pop-up colour opera windows and take a quiet walk around the block, there's a chance we'll buy cheaper. Smarter. Keep the car longer. And use it less.

Go back to the start of the chapter, where you figured out how much it was costing you to drive. Work out another figure: *if you saved just 10 percent of that, how much more could you invest in something that doesn't rust every year?*

Then use the interest table in chapter six to figure out how much wealthier you'd be when you retired.

Chapter 13

Divorce and Other Disasters: With All My Worldly Goods I Thee Split Fifty-Fifty

"There are far more songs about love than about divorce. Take a minute and think that over. Count up all the songs you know about love. Then count up all the divorce songs." Hoskins was about to make a point.

The only divorce song I could think of was the obvious one: "D-I-V-O-R-C-E."

"Aha!" Hoskins said. "There you have it. Makes you think the divorce lawyers are running the radio stations. Ninety percent of the songs on the air are about love. About a millionth of a percent are about divorce. If they were playing fair, they'd have to play one divorce song for every two love songs because about 50 percent of couples in this country end up splitting."

I'd read the statistics, too.

"It's all a plot by the divorce lawyers who run the stations. Sweet-talk you into marriage, then whammo! You end up paying big bucks to a divorce lawyer."

Hoskins was in the middle of wallpapering his bathroom ceiling, which may have been the reason divorce was on his mind. There was a large lump of paste on his forehead and a lot of hard gravel in his voice. There was also a three-foot-long piece of wallpaper from the ceiling drying on the bathroom mirror that I decided not to mention.

"And there are absolutely no songs about marriage contracts. If they don't do songs about marriage contracts, they should at the very least do warnings at the end of every love song. They could say something like, 'Warning: 50 percent of marriages end in divorce,' or, 'Marriage is a major contributor to divorce.' They have warnings on cigarette packs and a lot more people get married than smoke."

Hoskins stuck the last corner of the piece of paper he was working on to the ceiling and glared at it, daring it to peel as he slowly climbed down the stepladder he was working on. "It's time for a beer. I allow myself one beer per roll," he said.

Down in the kitchen he went deeper into the subject. "If I were King (a title Hoskins often assumes when he's frustrated), I'd pass a law. The law would say, 'Before anybody is allowed to get married, there has to be a marriage contract, a pre-nuptial agreement.'"

"Why a law?" I asked.

"Two reasons. First it would get rid of all that 'We're-so-much-in-love-it's-going-to-last-forever-so-we-don't-need-a-pre-nuptial-agreement' bullroar. *Everybody* would have to be party to an agreement, so there wouldn't be any about-to-be-brides or about-to-be-grooms asking their about-to-be-spouses why it was necessary in *their* case, or thinking that the bride or groom was getting married with the idea of divorce on her or his mind. Make the agreements mandatory in every case. That way, nobody would have to explain why they thought it was a sensible idea and there'd be no embarrassment."

"Second reason?"

"Divorce cost the country a lot of money. Because there are no pre-nuptial agreements we're paying a lot of judges to spend a lot of time deciding what the agreement should have been in retrospect. And we're paying a lot of money out to single parents who need government subsidies that they might not have needed if there were mandatory pre-nuptial agreements."

"So, do you have a pre-nuptial agreement?"

"Hell, I got married before they invented them." He took a sip of his beer. "I even got married before they invented divorces."

Two sets of screwdrivers

Divorces are *bad* financial planning. A divorced couple can't live as cheaply as a married one, because all of a sudden they're trying to afford two of a lot of things they only used to need one of: two kitchens, two living rooms, two cars, two sets of screwdrivers, two cable television subscriptions, two telephones, two can openers … Even vacations are more expensive; the package travel companies charge "single supplements."

I'm not a lawyer. Even if I were, explaining divorce law would be impossible in a book this size. Plus, particular laws are different in particular provinces or states. What's true in province or state may not be true in another, and what was true of divorce law 10 years ago may not be true today.

You need a lawyer. As Hoskins points out, you need one before you get married. It's a lot cheaper to agree on things then, than to fight about things later. And I believe that it would cut down on a lot of the fussing and fighting I've seen between couples arguing about who pays for what. Or even who mows the lawn and who does the dishes.

Getting a divorce also means you need a lawyer. Worse, it means you need two and are going to have to pay for two. Although I've run into two divorced couples in my life both of whom got tired of their *lawyers* arguing about things and went to a third lawyer. In front of the third lawyer they divided everything up and decided on who saw the kids when in matter of hours. Then they took *that* agreement and told their own lawyers that's what they were sticking to. They saved bundles on legal bills, although the original lawyers in both cases were less than pleased.)

Increasingly, getting a divorce means seeing your financial advisor. I've had quite a few couples visit me on these occasions and I think it works out quite well. It can get rid of a lot of financial illusions. Both people get a good solid view of the assets the couple is dividing. Both get a true idea of the liabilities they owe as a couple. And both can explore a number of different ways to split what's there so that the financial downside for both is reduced. For example, I've shown couples how *not* selling the family home and splitting the proceeds would save them both money. That's sometimes hard, because when both people have an emotional interest in the house, there tends to be some emotional blindness towards the financial aspects.

Divorce means seeing your financial advisor for other reasons, too. You're going to have to set up your own financial life differently. Your contributions to your various financial plans are going to change. You may have to switch financial tactics for a while because the pile of financial assets you had is now only half a pile—and that has a definite and disturbing impact on how soon and how well you can retire.

Another reason to see a financial advisor: you'll both be in the same room discussing the same issues. To me, that makes more sense than seeing two people in two rooms and perhaps discussing the financial issues in two different ways.

I don't want to get into an argument with lawyers—they are, after all, trained to argue—but I believe that seeing your financial advisor before scampering out to consult legal advisers is a good idea. As I've said, it strips away the financial illusions about what divorce means. It can settle financial arguments, which are a major cause of family strife. If it does both those things, who knows, it might even lead to reconciliation.

After all that, I have to tell you that I'm not a marriage counsellor. All I can handle is money.

Because that's what financial advisors do, we're also good people to see *before* you say "I do." We can show you a number of ways that marriage saves you money— beyond the facts that you'll be paying less each on accommodations and vacations, and because you only need one set of screwdrivers. You can set up spousal retirement plans, which can cut taxes. Some people may want to cut some pension plan contributions on the grounds that two can retire more cheaply than one—if they stay married.

You'll also want to name new insurance beneficiaries, draw up new wills, take another look at your disability insurance, and change your wealth-creation or wealth-protection strategies. If all this seems unromantic, let me assure you that it's a lot more romantic doing it before the event than doing it after. Each of you will know where you stand, what assets your marriage is backed with, and what liabilities you may be sharing.

The greatest instant benefit I ever saw a couple gain when they discussed their plans with a financial advisor happened when the pair mentioned to him that they'd set their marriage date for January 3. He was an incorrigible unromantic and ordered them to have it four days earlier. "That way you get the income tax deduction for the whole previous year."

One last reason to visit a financial advisor before heading down the aisle: you may get a good basis for the financial part of the pre-nuptial agreement Hoskins insists that every couple should have.

Chapter 14

The Last Third of Your Life: Retirement

I'm not even sure if you should retire. It turns a lot of people into bores.

Consider the prospect. You're sixty-something. You've been working 2,000 hours a year for 35 to 40 years. Suddenly you're looking at twenty-something years with over 2,000 hours a year freed up.

Twenty years is the same sweet space of time as there was between when you were 20 and when you hit 40. It's the same space you had between 40 and 60.

Mull it over. Think of how much you accomplished in one of those two-decade chunks of time. Count the people you fell in and out of love with, the bright accomplishments you made, the sheer number of things you got done.

You should come to the conclusion that it's too long a time to go without a definite plan. It's too long just to spend tying flies or ditzing in the garden. It's too long to spend parked in front of the television *caring* about whether Mimi's ex-husband Bob who's just run off with the wealthy stockbroker who doesn't know that she has terminal dyspepsia and who has a secret son engaged in an incestuous affair with …

Hell, even one week of afternoon television is too much.

What are you going to do with the last third of you life?

A lot of people spend the time torturing their spouses. A retired woman I know told me about her experiences when her husband joined her in retirement. He had nothing to do. So he began helping around the house, giving her good advice on the best way to vacuum efficiently taken from the days when he was a plant manager at a large manufacturing facility and an expert in time-and-motion studies. He'd help do the shopping, comparing the unit prices on dog food to find the best buy. Then he'd discuss the unit prices on the various dog foods as though he were discussing a quote on 14 tonnes of extruded aluminum.

Being an aware and sensitive man, he'd do his share of the housework. He'd clean the windows. He had been a very meticulous executive. Now he was very meticulous about cleaning the windows. He'd do it slowly so he wouldn't miss any spots. The house would be full of the slow, squeaking sound for very long periods of time.

The squeaking sound didn't bother him.

She went outside. He started to do the outside windows.

They avoided divorce. He promised to take up community work. She found a paint-and-wallpaper shop that needed part-time bookkeeping.

What are you going to do with the last third of *your* life?

A Plan Stolen From an Expert

Sydney Hunt is the delightful author of *How to Live in the Caribbean*. The book *used* to be called *How to Retire in the Caribbean*, but Mr. Hunt changed it. I like to think that part of the reason was to get away from the idea of retirement as a time in life when you just sit in the La-Z-Boy and watch your clock run down.

Mr. Hunt—aside from being delightful—is intelligent. He knew that a retirement—like a career and like a financial strategy—has to be *planned*. And he did more: he figured out *how* to plan it.

The idea—like so many brilliant ideas—is simple. Both you and your partner make up two lists, keeping them secret from each other.

The first list is all the things you never want to do again, like wear a suit, or shovel snow, or clean the oven, or be stuck in traffic jams. For a few weeks, you keep adding to list as you keep confronting the things you never want to do again.

At the same time, you start a second list. It's the list of things you *want* to do and have never had the chance to do because of your career. Things like run away and join the carnival, learn a new language, build a boat, live in a small town. You also keep this list secret from your partner.

Then, put both the "Wanna" and "Don't-ever-wanna-again" lists in order of your priorities.

What happens next is the tricky part. You and your partner should find some leisurely hours in a relaxing place and compare lists—without making comments, without getting into arguments. You're simply trying to share each other's objectives for the last third of your life. According to Mr. Hunt, you'll find out that a lot of what's on both of your lists will coincide. At the top of Mr. Hunt's "Don't-ever-wanna-again" list was "I hope I will never again attend a cocktail party." At the top of Mrs. Hunt's list was "I never again want to entertain your clients."

Comparing the lists will tell you a lot about your retirement. It told the Hunts that they were headed to the Caribbean. (He never wanted arthritis pain again; she didn't want to drive in snow.) Your lists may tell you you'd be happier in a downtown condo in Toronto or in a farmhouse near Boise, Idaho. And those are things you might never have found out if you hadn't undertaken Mr. Hunt's retirement exercise.

Mr. Hunt's Lists

You	*Your partner*
"I never again want to"	*"I never again want to"*

1 _____   _____
2 _____   _____
3 _____   _____
4 _____   _____
5 _____   _____
6 _____   _____
7 _____   _____
8 _____   _____
9 _____   _____
10 _____   _____

"I always wanted to"	*"I always wanted to"*
1_____	_____
2_____	_____
3_____	_____
4_____	_____
5_____	_____
6_____	_____
7_____	_____
8_____	_____
9_____	_____
10_____	_____

Financing the Last Third

You're not going to be going to work. So you won't need the same kind of clothing. You probably won't spend as much on gas. You may eat out less. You'll have time to do more around the house than you had before retiring.

So retirement can cost you less each month.

On the other hand, it can cost you more. Are you going to travel? Where? How? And how much does that cost? Are you going to take up new hobbies and what are their price tags?

In chapter 16 there's some comprehensive lists designed for budgeting. You should fill them out *twice:* once for your lifestyle before you retire, and once for the lifestyle you'll have *after*. Some people find they need only 50 percent of the income they had before retirement to enjoy life. A more normal figure is about 75 percent.

Which raises the question of whether you have enough money. If you follow the basics in this book, you should. But if you're depending on the government to fund your retirement, forget it—unless you're a civil servant with one of those plump, nicely indexed pensions. Governments are getting more generous—slightly. But depending on government plans alone will likely mean you had better develop a high tolerance for Kraft Dinner and bologna.

It's best to figure out what you're retirement income will be from all sources well before you retire. If the figure's too low, you're going to have to make adjustments to the way you live. You might have to move into smaller quarters. You may have to give up the idea of having two cars, or even one. You may be taking the bus to Florida instead of the jet to Tobago. But you should make those adjustments early. Otherwise, 10 years down the road you'll have even less to spend.

Five years before you retire isn't too early to call in your financial planner. I've known people who've done it 15 years in advance and have had a much, much healthier retirement because of it. Your financial planner should be able to help you through your Retirement Income Statement and it should look something like this.

Income from	You	Your partner
Retirement plan	_____	_____
Mutual funds	_____	_____
Annuities	_____	_____
Company pension	_____	_____
CPP	_____	_____
Social Security	_____	_____
Other Income		
Rent	_____	_____
Royalties	_____	_____
Part-time work	_____	_____
Total	_____	_____

Compare the total to the total for your desired life-style. If you're making more than you're spending, don't get too happy about it yet. Remember that although you may have stopped working, inflation's still on the job. The shirt that costs you $20 today may cost you $40 seven years from now. If you're not going to be making as much as you'd wanted to spend …

Sorry.

That's life for most retired individuals. And I do not believe that it's going to get much better. The population is greying rapidly and a much larger part of it will be depending on government pensions to get by. In the next 20 to 30 years there will be a lower percentage of the population working. So, although there will be more people taking money out, there will be relatively fewer putting money in.

That doesn't argue in favour of big increases in government pensions. And it will also put some strain on private pension plans.

Another Reason to Call the Financial Advisor

Retirement plan regulations change. Tax rules change. The kinds of investments open to retired people change. And your situation isn't the same as anybody else's. You need *specific* advice about creating a Retirement Income Fund. You need to know about the tax implications of delving into your Retirement funds.

Am I making this sound complicated? It is.

And all these things are too important to decide in an afternoon. After all, you're planning the last third of your life.

Here's what I suggest.

1. Make an appointment with your financial advisor. Bring in all the pieces of paper you have filed away under "Retirement": the pension benefit brochures, the Retirement Plan reports—everything to help your financial advisor determine your retirement income.
2. Talk to the advisor about your options. Make notes—lots of notes.
3. Have your financial advisor go out into the marketplace. Ask him or her to get multiple quotes on annuities to compare the kinds of income they will generate. Some are better than others. Ask your advisor about income options; they need to be as carefully matched to your specific needs as any other kind of investment. Have the planner work out your likely tax situation with each type of solution.
4. Tell the advisor what you think—now that you've had time to understand and educate yourself about what's happening in the market at this time. Ask all your questions. Make sure you get them thoroughly answered and that both you and your partner understand it all.
5. *Then* make your financial retirement plan.

Hold on, you aren't through yet. Remember, way back towards the beginning we said that financial planning was a lifelong process. It *continues* after retirement: you just can't shift your financial affairs into automatic pilot.

Chapter 15

Your Will: If a Piano Falls on You Tomorrow, What Happens to Your Family?

If you're not going to make a will in the next month, please sign the following document:

I, _____, of _____, being of sound mind and body, have nevertheless decided not to make a will. I understand that this will be of huge financial inconvenience to my family.

First, it will tie up all assets for what could be a considerable length of time and could mean that they may have to go to the bank to borrow money to support themselves until the whole mess is cleared up. There's a good chance that they may have to borrow money for my funeral.

Second, it will vastly increase the legal bills involved because although a will can cost under $100 to make, settling an estate where there is no will can cost thousands.

Third, it will take my survivors months of meetings to sort things out. This will really tick them off and cause them to think that I was a turkey. And they'll be right. And they'll tell their friends that I was a turkey, too.

Fourth, I realize that by not making a will, I'm leaving a lot of decisions in the hands of the provincial government, which is not famous for making fabulous decisions. I'm aware that the Official Guardian will likely dole out to my children any money they think the children should have until the children come of age.

Fifth, by not making a will to let the authorities know where I want my money to go, it's fairly likely that some of the money will go to the people who don't need it—at the expense of people who do. Or it'll go to people I don't like, and they'll laugh at me all the way to the bank.

Sixth, by not making a will I do not give myself the chance to donate my organs to patients who need them. Somebody who might have been able to see if I'd made my will clear, will stay blind longer.

Signed _____
Date _____
Get your spouse or a close friend to witness here: _____

By procrastinating instead of making a will, you're really deciding to do everything listed in the "non-will" above.

Graydon G. Watters, who wrote a detailed and intelligent book on personal financial planning, tells the story of a man he calls Doug who lived in Kitchener, Ontario. Doug fell, suffered a concussion, and died at the age of 44. Doug *had* a will, but it was nine years old and had been made when he was married to his first wife. He hadn't made a new will. Result: his assets went to his first wife.

I've known several people—men and women—who have died without wills. The result uniformly has been long, expensive, and painful meetings with lawyers and civil servants. In every case, no matter how much the family loved "the dear deceased," the memory was considerably blemished.

You can decide to make a will right now. You can put down this book and phone your lawyer to make an appointment to do it. Go now. I'll wait. I'm in no hurry.

If you haven't done what I told you, go make the phone call now.

What You Have Got to Decide: If You Can't Take It With You, Who's Going to Get It?

First, you have to decide on an executor or executrix. The decisions you make in your will won't happen by magic. Someone has to make them happen, and that's the executor/executrix's job. You *can* get a trust company to handle the chore, but the trust company may charge you a percentage of your total estate. It's preferable, and cheaper, to have a close friend do it. Make a deal that if your friend dies first, you'll be his or her executor and vice-versa. By doing this, you may have done your friend the additional favour of convincing him or her to make a will.

Make decisions about your funeral and how it will be paid for. That'll spare your family several hours of depressing conversation.

If both you and your spouse die, who'll look after your children? Have you contacted your choice of guardians to make sure they're up to the job? Decide how the expenses of raising the children should be paid. What do you leave your bartender, your hairdresser, your next-door neighbour?

What special gifts do you want to give your friends and relations? Who gets your fishing rods or your antique earrings? What should be done with your clothes? You should know that giving these gifts may have some tax implications to the person who receives them. This is something to discuss with your lawyer or financial planner.

Do you want a sum of money left to a specific charity, to your university, to a club you belong to, to the library you borrow books from?

Do you want to delay giving gifts or bequests until you die? There may be good reasons to make the gift while you're alive. Again, there may be tax implications.

How are you going to make sure your family is taken care of? Will you put your money in a trust where assets are transferred, but you decide how the assets will be managed? A trust can let you take a certain stock you own, put it into the hands of a trustee for management, and have the proceeds go to a child's education, for example. Your lawyer or a good financial planner will tell you about other examples and should tell you about trusts that you can create while you're alive.

You Don't Make a Will and Forget It

Your assets change. Children grow up. You start to have grandchildren. Your favourite charity changes.

Think about how you would have made a will if you'd done it five years ago. (If you have an existing will, this is probably a good time to look at it.) Now, think about how things have changed in the past five years.

Would your children need more money—or less?

Would your spouse still be comfortable with what was left?

Would the same person still be named as the children's guardian?

Which beneficiaries would have changed?

Have your assets gone up and should they be disposed of differently?

Every five years is not too often to review your will. If your estate's large, you may want to review it annually.

What Happens if the Piano Falls on Your Head and You Live?

If you haven't planned properly, you can be just as much of a turkey in a hospital bed as you can in a coffin.

But you *have* planned. You've given your spouse or *someone* your power of attorney, right? Because if you haven't and the piano falls on your head and you slip into a three-year coma, things are going to be hard to manage. Suppose your spouse had to sell the house to pay the bills while you were in hospital? How would s/he do that if you're not able to sign the papers? Suppose your stocks are dropping on the markets? How does your spouse prevent further losses? How does your spouse get access to your bank account to pay the mortgage? How does your spouse tell your Retirement Plan people to keep your money in growth stocks instead of sticking it in low-grade paper?

Without a power of attorney your spouse or friends may have their hands tied.

Time to see the lawyer or your financial advisor, right?

Good thing you've already made an appointment.

Chapter 16

Every Journey of a Thousand Miles
Begins With a Few Blisters

"You're writing a book, are you?" said Hoskins.

I was all excited. The publisher tells me that most first and second-time writers are. I told Hoskins how I'd bought a special recording machine so that I could dictate notes in my car. Then I told him about the great deal I'd gotten on a new computer that I could sit in the special area I'd set aside in my den. And I told him about the special mini lap top computer I'd bought so I could write when I was on airplanes and in hotel rooms.

"Heavens," he said. "Imagine Shakespeare getting along with only a pen."

I ignored him. It's something I'm trying to become good at. He went on anyway. "I remember when I was trying to get my weight down. I bought this special diet book that told you that everything you'd ever liked was 300 calories more than you needed. And I'd special chart with a daily diet plan that went up on the refrigerator door which let you fill in what you'd actually eaten with a special grease pencil. I went to Dowd's Sporting Goods and bought a set of those dumb-bells because I not only wanted a *thin* body, I wanted a *toned* body. I got all this stuff together over a period of about three days and then this geezer comes over and says to me, 'Do you have the shovel out of the garage yet.' I asked the geezer what he meant and he said, 'Eventually, if you want to get the snow off the walk you gotta quit buying equipment and get the shovel out of the garage.'"

That night, I finally plugged the computer in and started writing. I got the shovel out of the garage.

The 50-day Plan

People buy an awful lot of books on financial planning, how to get rich, and how to save money. Check the best-seller list: usually there's a book on it telling you how to get your financial act together. In a lot of cases I think the major financial benefits these books deliver are to the writer and the publisher, because the reader never gets the shovel out of the garage. They read all the good advice, look at the nice charts, take out their calculators, and do some figuring—but the damn shovel stays in the damn garage.

The financial advice isn't taken. Which means the financial benefits never happen.

That makes me angry, and it should probably make you angry, too, because you've just paid out good money for this book. *How do we change the situation so that you actually do start leading a financially fit life?*

Psychologists say that it takes 40 to 50 days to change any habit. So I've put together a 50-day plan. It has several advantages.

It doesn't require that you do a lot of work all at once. In fact, it should only require that you spend a couple of hours a week. You should set a time and a space aside for those two hours. Make an appointment with yourself.

A second advantage is that it's easy on the conscience. There's no need to browbeat yourself or anyone else about past transgressions.

That's good, because as I've mentioned before, there's somebody else who has to come to the meeting: your spouse. The government estimates that there are as many women working in the labour force as men. Put it another way, the partnership is now equal when it comes to the numbers of both sexes working. Because of employment equity legislation across the country, wage levels are converging as well. The days when "he makes the money and she spends it" are over, and they should have ended long ago.

You're both affected.

You both have to make the decisions.

You both have to agree with them.

You both have to know where every last dime is in case of premature death of disability.

And you both have to support the other's decisions, just as a good executive has to support a fellow executive making decisions in his/her area of responsibility. As a financial advisor, I've seen too many instances where one spouse knew how to cut down on household expenditures but the other sabotaged the effort by not understanding the objective or how it was to be reached. Keeping 50 percent of the executives of a company in the dark about decisions is a sure recipe for disaster. So is having 50 percent of a life partnership.

There's another thing I have to repeat. Getting into a sensible family plan does *not* start out by figuring out who's guilty of what. If a company's executives were involved in endless backbiting about who made the wrong decisions two years ago and who failed to do something six months ago, they'd never get on with planning for tomorrow. And the company would be belly up.

The answer is to pretend that you're both new executives of an old company. You've been brought in to turn the place around. You have new objectives. Get together with a calculator, pencils, a copy of this book, and a smile.

First week: The All-New (Your Name) Corporation

The first thing you have to do is to figure out where your company is financially. That means doing a lot a financial statement. That's simpler than doing your income tax.

(Your Name) Estimated Annual Income

	Person A	*Person B*	*Total*
Pay	_____	_____	_____
Bonuses	_____	_____	_____
Commission	_____	_____	_____
Other	_____	_____	_____
Family Allowance	_____	_____	_____
Pensions	_____	_____	_____
Investments	_____	_____	_____
Gifts	_____	_____	_____
Sales of goods			
Or property	_____	_____	_____
Money coming in	_____	_____	_____
Total	_____	_____	_____

(Your Name) Estimated Annual Spending

	Person A	*Person B*	*Total*
HOME			
Rent/Mortgage	_____	_____	_____
Property Taxes	_____	_____	_____
Insurance	_____	_____	_____
Repairs	_____	_____	_____
Decorating	_____	_____	_____
Heat	_____	_____	_____
Electricity	_____	_____	_____
Telephone	_____	_____	_____
Furniture	_____	_____	_____
Appliances	_____	_____	_____
FOOD			
Groceries	_____	_____	_____
Restaurants	_____	_____	_____
Pets	_____	_____	_____
CLOTHING			
Shoes	_____	_____	_____
Cleaning	_____	_____	_____

TRANSPORTATION
Transit　　　　　　_____　_____　_____
Car Payments　　 _____　_____　_____
Car Insurance　　 _____　_____　_____
License　　　　　 _____　_____　_____
Gas, oil, tires　　 _____　_____　_____
(see chapter 12)

PERSONAL
Hair　　　　　　 _____　_____　_____
Makeup　　　　　 _____　_____　_____
Hobbies　　　　　 _____　_____　_____
Movies　　　　　 _____　_____　_____
Plays　　　　　　 _____　_____　_____
Video rentals　　 _____　_____　_____
Education　　　　 _____　_____　_____
Clubs　　　　　　 _____　_____　_____
Memberships　　　 _____　_____　_____
Family Allowances _____　_____　_____
Christmas　　　　 _____　_____　_____
Birthdays　　　　 _____　_____　_____
Special Occasions _____　_____　_____
Vacations　　　　 _____　_____　_____

OTHER LEISURE
Boat　　　　　　 _____　_____　_____
Snowmobile　　　 _____　_____　_____
Cottage　　　　　 _____　_____　_____
Trailers　　　　　 _____　_____　_____
Sports　　　　　 _____　_____　_____
Rentals　　　　　 _____　_____　_____

GOVERNMENT
Income Tax　　　 _____　_____　_____
Health insurance　 _____　_____　_____

HEALTH/PENSION
RRSP　　　　　　 _____
Company pension plan_____　_____　_____
Dental plan　　　 _____　_____　_____

Health plan	_____	_____	_____
Dentist	_____	_____	_____
Optical	_____	_____	_____
Other	_____	_____	_____

What's Coming In Versus What's Going Out

Income	_____	_____	_____
Outflow	_____	_____	_____
Difference	_____	_____	_____

Well.

Sit and stare at that for a while. If you're like most people, you'll have some trouble coming to terms with it. Most people either over-estimate or under-estimate their expenditures. So you'll have to start making adjustments: "I forgot to put in that I buy two bottles of wine every week." Or, "Maybe the car costs more than I thought." Or, "We've got a money leak." Or, "How come if we're making all this money we don't have anything to show for it?"

Right.

This first step isn't about getting the details on your income and your outgoing correct down to the last penny. It's about getting a general picture of what your cash flow situation is so that you can begin to ask questions about how much you should be investing and how you should go about planning for your future priorities.

In most families, and in most relationships, one partner takes care of certain areas of spending while the other takes care of the rest. I take care of buying weekend groceries; my wife takes care of weekday groceries. She buys cleaning supplies and I buy those clips, connectors, and reverse pin irons that you have to get at the hardware store. She buys the household goods. I sign the cheques for insurance. She pays for the children's lessons. I buy snow tires.

Writing all this stuff down is embarrassing. It shows what a stereotype we tend to make between husband and wife. Let's leave that as it is for the moment. All we're trying to do here is change your financial life. Changing the rest of your life is probably covered in another book on another shelf.

One thing at a time.

After doing the first week's work, go and get two photocopies of it. On the sheet that covers expenditures, put a note beside each item that tells you which partner normally controls that expenditure. Then, give each other an objective. Each of you has to find a way to spend 10 percent less on those things your normally in charge of paying for or buying. If you don't normally buy the laundry detergent or the light bulbs, stay away from telling the partner in charge of laundry and light bulbs to buy bulk detergent at the warehouse or to switch every thing in the house over to 15 watts. If you're normally in charge of lawnmowers and vegetables, do the best job you can on those things. Some amounts—like health insurance and house taxes and insurance—can't be reduced. Some amounts can.

But always remember when doing any of these financial exercises that you're not trying to punish yourself. On the other hand, you're not trying to coddle yourself either. The best parallel I can think of is a medical situation. You have a problem. You can undergo some short-term pain and get it taken care of so that it will never bother you again in your life. Or you can decide that you'll pass on the short-term pain that an operation would bring. You'll take an aspirin instead, and when the "slight" problem you have now turns into a major problem later, you'll worry about it then.

Understandable. But I'd take the short-term pain in exchange for long-term gain.

End of sermon.

Back to work. You know what your objective is. Go do it before next week's meeting.

Second Week: The All-New (Your Name) Corporation

Since the last meeting you've ended up with two problems.

1. You and your partner started talking about money an awful lot. *Or* you stopped talking altogether because you were afraid of talking about money. You need some solutions to this problem or you're going to be back in the chapter on divorce. The first solution: only talk about money on the days you and your partner have your board meeting. Second solution: I *know* that talking about your family as a corporation is awfully cutesy, but it does give you the proper intellectual distance from the situation. Talking about what you're doing in the same terms you'd use to talk about busi-

ness problems keeps you from reminding your partner about the $53 that was spent on *somebody's* Australian bush hat last Saturday.

2. You've run into a brick wall. You're *committed* to car payments, daycare payments, credit card payments. You *can't* get out of them. So *how* are you going to reach your goal of paring 10 percent off the budget that you as an executive are corporately responsible for? The answer is that maybe you can't in the short term; although, I've gone through this exercise with hundreds of clients who found that they could—if they really wanted to.

The exercise may have proven that your corporation's long-term ability to survive and prosper is hedged in by debt: the car, the plastic, the irreducible whatever. You can reduce the amounts you spend on groceries, hardware, meals, and entertainment, but the other stuff you're contracted for. You can't reduce the car payments, for example, until the car payments have run their course. *Then* you can reduce them.

Ok.

That brings us to the objective of our second corporate meeting. The agenda looks like this.

1. Review of last meeting.
2. Plans by partner A on which expenditures can be immediately reduced and how close this is to the target of 10 percent.
3. Partner B congratulates Partner A on the hard work and thought that went into the plans.
4. Plan by Partner B on what expenditures can be reduced and how close this is to the target of 10 percent.
5. Partner A congratulates Partner B.
6. Partner A and Partner B decide to give each other and *themselves* a contract, stating that they will reduce these expenditures so they can get off the darn topic and get on with life.

"I, Partner A, as a result of meeting on _____ have stated my objective to reduce expenditures in those areas I am responsible for by $_____ per month."

Signed:_____

"I, Partner B, as a result of meeting on _____ have stated my objective to reduce expenditures in those areas I am responsible for by $_____ per month."
Signed:_____

Signing these contracts may seem a little childish. That's where I got the idea: a very progressive private school that charges parents substantial sums to teach their children how to really *learn*. At this school they don't nag kids to get their homework done or to learn binomial theorems. At the beginning of the week, the teacher goes to each pupil and asks what each feels up to learning in the coming week. The pupil writes it down and signs it. Stuff gets learned. Confrontation is minimized. Life is happy, but what needs doing gets done. Sign the contract. Tuck it where you keep your credit cards. Make another copy; put it in your cheque book.

In the same way, having an agenda—like some of the ones that follow—may seem like a silly idea. It isn't. That's why companies have agendas. The president of your credit card company has an agenda. The president of the company that runs your bank has an agenda. The president of the company that sells you your insurance has an agenda. The reasons are simple: agendas stop people from getting off topic. They make sure all the bases have been covered.

"They Have a Contract Out on You"

"They" refers to the mortgage company, the people who have given you the privilege of having a nice credit card, the life insurance company, the friendly folks at the Canada Customs and Revenue Agency, and the bright, smiling people in the loans office. For the third meeting you're responsible for bringing together the bits and pieces of paper describing how much money you owe within your areas of corporate responsibility.

There's an upside. You should also being all of the documents dealing with your assets: stocks, bonds, retirement plan, business assets, savings accounts, and so forth.

Third Week: The All-New (Your Name) Corporation

Let's get the tough stuff over with first.

The (Your Name) Corporation Debt

Credit card A _____

Credit card B _____

Credit card C _____

Credit card D _____

Credit card E _____

Others _____

Loan A _____

Loan B _____

Loan C _____

Loan D _____

Loan E _____

Income tax due _____

Mortgage A _____

Mortgage B _____

Life insurance loans _____

Total _____

Throughout the book I've been telling you how much money *you* could earn by investing it. Most of the time, figuring it out has been fairly easy. You just simply turn to the compound interest table in chapter six, figure out the going interest rate, figure out how many years you're going to have it invested, and you'll know how much you'll make.

People who loan you money are investing it in *you*. You provide their growth and their profit. Take each of the loans above. Remember the interest rate. Remember how long you'll have to go on paying. Then figure out how much you *really* have to end up paying on each debt before you're free.

	Current Amount	*Interest*	*Total payments*
Credit card A	_____	_____	_____
Credit card B	_____	_____	_____
Credit card C	_____	_____	_____
Credit card D	_____	_____	_____
Credit card E	_____	_____	_____
Others	_____	_____	_____
Loan A	_____	_____	_____
Loan B	_____	_____	_____
Loan C	_____	_____	_____
Loan D	_____	_____	_____

Loan E	_____	_____	_____
Income tax due	_____	_____	_____
Mortgage A	_____	_____	_____
Mortgage B	_____	_____	_____

This *can* be depressing. Although, one client of mine was very cheered up when he saw the chart: "You mean I can have *that* many credit cards and *that* many loans?" he said. He was a little unclear about the concept of what we're trying to do here.

What we're trying to do is pound home the idea that a credit card is a debit card. The credit card companies are making money at about 1½ percent per month as I write this. If *you* could invest at 1½ percent per month, you'd be an extremely happy camper.

The mortgage company is making money off its investment in you, as is the loan company, and all the rest of those organizations. *And the money they're making is money you can't invest.* It's money that will disappear from your life forever. And most of it is money that you'll have to pay for with after-tax dollars, which means that if you're paying income tax at a 30 percent level, you actually have to earn $1.30 to pay off the debt.

Plus the interest.

Now, your job for the next meeting is to figure out how you can cut down on this financial haemorrhaging. Start with figuring out how to cut down on your credit card: they charge the most interest. Some people hide them in safety deposit boxes. Some people give them to friends to hide for them until they really, really need them. I know one man who mailed his credit cards to his uncle in Fresno, California.

And some people just cut them up with scissors.

Whatever.

But get as many as possible of them retired, hidden, burned, or put in the blender. And then do *not* just pay the monthly minimum—pay as much as you can. You're making 19 percent on your money every time you pay off an extra dollar on your credit card. And 19 percent is a whale of a lot to be paying.

Fourth Week: The All-New (Your Name) Corporation

The agenda goes like this:

1. Review of last meeting.
2. Report by Partner A on how cutting expenditures by 10 percent is proceeding. Specific examples are given.
3. Report by Partner B on how cutting expenditures is proceeding. Specific examples are given.
4. Report by Partner A on ideas to cut and repay certain liabilities. Target dates are given.
5. Report by Partner B on ideas to cut and repay certain liabilities. Target dates are given, and the following contract is filled out.

	Liability to be repaid	*Target date*
Debt 1	_____	_____
Debt 2	_____	_____
Debt 3	_____	_____
Debt 4	_____	_____
Debt 5	_____	_____
Debt 6	_____	_____
Debt 7	_____	_____
Debt 8	_____	_____
Debt 9	_____	_____
Debt 10	_____	_____

Signed: _____

And: _____

(Obviously, you have to be realistic in your schedule. Nothing kills a dieter's ambition faster than to find out that s/he can't be "swimsuit sleek" by getting rid of 30 pounds in 30 days in order to look good for the beach. Be realistic: remember you're an executive of a corporation here.)

6. Discussion of assets.
Your corporation's assets

REAL ESTATE
Home _____
Cottage _____
Other _____

OTHER FIXED ASSETS
Business   _____
Club shares   _____
Other   _____

SEMI-LIQUID ASSETS
Mutual funds   _____
Stocks   _____
Bonds   _____
Cars   _____
Mortgages owed you   _____
Retirement Funds   _____
Annuities   _____
Others   _____

LIQUID ASSETS
Cash   _____
Life insurance cash value   _____
Savings certificates   _____
Others   _____

OTHER ASSETS
Furniture   _____
Jewellery   _____
Antiques   _____
Coins   _____
Other   _____
Total   _____

Net worth statement:
Total assets: $_____
Total debt: $_____
Equals net worth: $_____

For a 25-year-old couple, a net worth figure that's a *minus* may not be a bad sign.

After all, they've just begun their accumulation of assets. They may have purchased a house that's put them $150,000 in debt, but which is gaining in equity 10 percent every year.

For a 45-year-old couple, the same net worth figure could be cause for concern, depending on their asset mix.

For a 55-year-old couple, it's likely a disaster.

In some cases a financial planner could look at a young couple with a $25,000 net worth and decide it's too *much*. The couple *should* have some debt in a house, a recreational property, or a business. They should be taking on leveraged debt in order to make more money later.

It changes from person to person, couple to couple, and year-to-year.

You'll need to prepare for the fifth week's meeting. The best way to do that is to read ahead.

Week Five: The All-New (Your Name) Corporation: Where's It Going?

You know how much you spend.

And you know how much you make.

You know how much you owe.

And how much is owed to you.

You have target objectives to cut spending. And target objectives to cut debt.

In short, you know how you can improve your situation over the next weeks and months. But what's the ultimate goal? Or even next year's goal?

Here's a list of typical goals people set for themselves. Tick off the ones you're interested in.

	Priority	*Date*	*Cost*
Children			
Sending children to university			
Buying a car			
Buying a home			
Buying a vacation Home			

Buying investment			
Property	_____	_____	_____
Renovating	_____	_____	_____
An expensive			
vacation	_____	_____	_____
Major			
appliances	_____	_____	_____
Boat	_____	_____	_____
Early retirement	_____	_____	_____
Other	_____	_____	_____

Obviously, all of these things cost money. If you're like me, and most other Canadians, you'd have to undertake that list one item at a time. Go back over the list and write down which ones you'd do first, which one second, and so forth. You may find yourself having to do trade offs with your partner ("okay, we'll make renovation number five if the boat can be number six").

Then as a further exercise in reality therapy, put a year down beside each item.

And *then* as a further exercise in reality therapy, put down the price.

What you're going to find is that the chart you and your partner have just put together will require you to make even more trade offs. You can't but an $18,000 boat when you've just bought a $22,000 car. And buying either of those may mean that you don't have a hope of buying a $150,000 condo for a long time to come.

The chart's an attitude adjuster. You'll find yourself saying things like: "We'll settle for a $10,000 car and a $10,000 boat and we can have both," or "We'll get the $10,000 car and wait two more years for the boat," or "We'll rent a darn boat, buy a used car, and use the money we save over the next two years to add to our savings and invest in the condo." (You'll notice that in all of this *nobody* says, "We'll wait until after we pay off the car to borrow for the boat." That's because our first decision has been to save ahead for three years so that we don't have to take a loan for our first priority because we'd rather be making interest than paying interest.)

From your chart you can begin making a long-term financial plan. But let's leave that until meeting six. In the meantime, put a copy of your chart where you can both see it every night and every morning. It'll keep you thinking.

Week 6: The (Your Name) Corporation's Long-Term Plan

People change. Yesterday's hippy is today's yuppie and tomorrow's retiree. Because people change, their plans change. When you were 20 (or 30 or 40 or ...), did you plan on being where you are and doing what you do today? I didn't. I was going to be centre forward for the Detroit Red Wings, making half a million a year on testimonials *alone*, and living in a penthouse with ...

That was, of course, before I became the mature, intellectual, sensitive person you see before you today.

Despite the fact that people and their plans change, *it's vital to have a long-range plan.*

Reason one: it gives you a direction. It's hard to know which way to point the boat unless you know you want to end up in Rio. Similarly, it's hard to work up the will power to start investing in mutual funds unless you know you want to end up in Rio. Similarly, it's hard to work up the will power to start investing in mutual funds unless you know your ultimate objective is not to be living on bologna after you're 65.

Reason two for making a long-term plan: it gives you a context to put all your short-term plans in order. If you know the boat's ultimately heading for Rio, and that you'd like to hit Australia, Portugal, San Francisco, and Vancouver along the way, the long-term plan tells you how much time you need for the trip.

Reason three: it's enjoyable. Planning long-term goals is fun. You get to explore your partner's psyche and your own. You may discover that you both share the common goal of living in a little grass shack on the beach and can skip buying the monster house in order to start beachcombing 10 years earlier.

Order we want things in	*Time to Save for*	*Acquisition date*
1.		
2.		
3.		
4.		
5.		
6.		
7.		
8.		
9.		
10.		

This chart's easy to fill in. You've already traded off priorities between the partners in the (Your Name) Corporation, so you know "The Order We Want Things In." Because the previous meetings have put a cost against most of those things, and because you know how much money is coming in and going out, you know how long it'll take to save for each part of your long-range plan. So if you stick to your guns, you should know what date you should be able to acquire everything you're setting out to get.

There are some warnings that come along with this list.

First, (am I boring you with this?) you have to save yourself from temptation. Don't borrow to pay for things like cars and vacations. The reason's obvious. When you buy a $20,000 car that you pay cash for, you pay $20,000. Actually, you pay less because while *saving* for the car, you've been earning interest on your money. *But,* when you spread out your payments over three years, you end up paying at least $30,000 because of the compound interest. Result: you've paid $10,000 more and the result of *that* is that you're $10,000 behind on the next step of your plan. And that delays the step after that, and ...

So when you're buying a car too early, talk to each other. Ask if buying one thing early is worth delaying nine other things. Ask each other if there's an alternative: a smaller car, a used car, a car that's both small and used.

Usually, the excuse for buying early is, "Boy, I really deserve this!" Maybe. But do you deserve to have all those other things delayed because of it? Are you playing fair with the rest of (Your Name) Corporation?

Second warning: plans fall apart. People get sick. The economy gets sick. The housing market blasts off. People are laid off. *None of these things is an excuse to abandon the plan.* Don't give up: adjust. Delay priorities. Downsize projects. Do what the corporations do.

Third warning: base everything on your *current* income and don't fall into the "I'll-get-a-raise-by-then" trap. You may indeed get a raise. In which case you can speed up the plan. On the other hand, you know an awful lot of people who have lost their jobs during the last five years—during *any* last five years—and some of those people lost their jobs for reasons beyond their control. Even—bless us—the civil service has had caps put on salary increases. And in any case, whatever raise you get may just keep you even with inflation and tax increases.

Fourth warning: you still have to "pay-yourself-first." You still have invested in mutual funds. You still have to be putting money into your Retirement Plan. Otherwise, unless your ultimate goal is to work until you drop or live in poverty, which is all that government pension plans really add up to, you're kidding yourself.

Week Seven: The All-New (Your Name) Corporation

Hey. You notice something?

You and your partner are beginning to talk about finances in a pretty mature way. You're beginning to share goals. You're starting to realize how you can both get what you want by working together. You have a much better understanding of your total financial situation and you feel more in control.

So what's left to do?

There are a number of things. Companies just don't set up plans once and then forget them. They monitor those plans constantly to see whether objectives are really being achieved.

It's obvious that to continue *recording* successes, you have to continue *having* successes. Seven weeks is a nice start, but it is *only* a start. What we have to do now is decide how to ensure that you'll continue to reap the rewards of planning.

Here's what I suggest.

Continue to hold your weekly meetings. Don't just *say* you're going to do it. Take time right now to promise each other on what specific day of the week you're going to do it.

At the end of this section there's an agenda for each weekly meeting. Sometimes you'll find you can whiz through this agenda in five minutes. At other times, you're going to have to take a couple of hours. Commit to taking the time. In the end, for most people it's the most highly paid work they'll do all week. It's worth more than double-overtime.

At the end of this section you'll also find a series of additional topics of your future meetings. These topics come form the chapters on Retirement Plans, Insurance, Mutual Funds, Financial Advisors, and Wills. *You're now in shape to start considering those things in detail.*

Your Weekly Meeting Agenda

This meeting can usually happen in just 15 minutes. When you spend 40 hours a week making money—spending 1/64th of that time keeping track of it is well worthwhile.

1. Quick review of business from last week: things like whether you got in touch with the insurance salesperson or the mortgage company.
2. Quick review of liabilities. Week by week you should be able to complete this sentence: "We owe $_____$ less than last week, and $_____$ less than last month and $_____$ less than the same week last year." You'll find that filling out that sentence is very motivating—something like the motivation a successful dieter gets from being able to record regular losses. You'll help yourself with this process by having all the bills on hand. Keep all the last year's bills from each credit card company fastened to each other and you'll be able to make these quick comparisons. Similarly, keep your loan statements from each lender together.
3. Quick review of assets. Again, the objective is to complete a sentence. This time the sentence is: "We have $_____$ more in assets than we had last month, and $_____$ more than we had last year."
4. Review of investment success. The sentence to complete is: "We are $\_\_\_\_\_$ over (or under) our investment program this month."
5. Review of progress toward your next goal. "We have $_____$ to save until we attain our next goal. We will achieve it in _____ months."
6. New business. Go back to the table of contents for this book. Is there anything you should be doing? Calling the mutual fund people? Updating you will? Putting an extra payment on the mortgage? Who'll be responsible for seeing that that happens by your next meeting?

The best way I have sent these weekly meeting handled is to have each partner take turns at running them. This makes sure that each one is fully aware of what's going on—and that each one does the same amount of work.

If the idea of having a weekly meeting seems too much, remember that most successful small businesses go through the same kind of weekly meeting. And that between the two of you, you're making a hefty sum. It's worth the time to take care of it.

Additional Meeting Topics

1.   Will.
2.   Insurance.
3.   Retirement Plans.
4.   Financial advisor.
5.   Mutual funds.
6.   What's the plan when you renew your mortgage?
7.   Income tax.
8.   Next priority expenditure.
9.   How do we invest our bonuses?
10.   Which credit cards should we keep?

Draw your line from the first column to a subject in the second column, in order that the subjects are a priority for you. Before the meeting, prepare by re-reading the relevant subject matter in the book.

During the meeting, be calm. Smile. As the meetings go on, you should find yourself with more and more reasons to be calm. And more reasons to smile. If you're not getting richer, you're at least becoming less poor. And if you stick to it, you're going to be better off than 90 percent of most families.

Chapter 17

Students Who Know What Grades They're Getting, Perform Better Than Students Who Don't

There used to be a movement in the educational world not to let the students know what grades they were getting in school. At the time, it appeared to make sense. Giving grades puts pressure on kids. It can make some feel like failures and others feel as though they don't have to do as much work.

That was the theory. The reality was that when the teachers stopped giving grades the work of *all* the students slipped. They learned less.

This section is about giving yourself grades.

Remember your first bankbook? Remember how you put in your first deposit and felt a small innocent glow? And then you put in the second deposit and watched the amount climb? And then you started realizing that the two dollars you were putting in each week eventually amounted to something and that if you kept doing this for 20 weeks you'd end up with enough money to buy a bike?

This section is a bit like that—except that it's longer term. *Most people don't keep track of their investments, their assets, and their debts all in the same place.*

Companies do. And that's why companies usually perform better financially than most individuals. Simply having the report card makes you do better.

Your Debt Report Card

Check out the debt checklist in chapter 16. Consolidate the debt, and report it here. Your debts won't always go down. When you increase real assets like buying real estate by taking on a mortgage, they'll go up. However, if you control your purchasing of depreciating assets like cars, boats, and appliances, you won't be continuously adding to your debt. If you see that your debt report is going up because of those things year after year, it's time to sit down and have a long chat with yourself.

Date loan was taken out	*Amount of loan*	*Interest rate*	*Monthly payment*
_____	_____	_____	_____
_____	_____	_____	_____
_____	_____	_____	_____
_____	_____	_____	_____
_____	_____	_____	_____
_____	_____	_____	_____
_____	_____	_____	_____
Total	_____	_____	_____

Your Retirement Plan Report Card

Obviously, your Retirement Plan's should grow in value every year, both because you've made your maximum contribution, and because you've decided on the right investments within it.

Year	*Your Value*	*Partner's value*	*Contributions this year*
_____	_____	_____	_____
_____	_____	_____	_____
_____	_____	_____	_____
_____	_____	_____	_____
_____	_____	_____	_____
_____	_____	_____	_____
_____	_____	_____	_____
Total	_____	_____	_____

Your Mutual Fund Report Card

This should be calculated annually. A keen awareness of how your mutual funds are performing from year to year will allow you to sleep a lot easier. Remember, mutual funds are long-term investments.

Name of Fund	Number of Shares Invested	Original Amount	Unit Price	Current value
1.				
2.				
3.				
4.				
5.				
6.				
7.				
8.				
9.				
10.				
Total				

Your Real Estate Report Card

This requires a bit of honesty—and a bit of snooping around. Whenever there's a home for sale in your area, phone and find out what the asking price is. That will give you an idea of what your own real estate is worth. Want a better idea? Check with your local real estate board for the average home price in your area. That will also give you an idea.

Year	Average price in area	Price of our house

Your Other Assets Report Card

You're only allowed to list assets that you absolutely, definitely, positively, no-kidding could sell. At the price you could sell them at. Check the asset list in chapter 16 for guidance. And don't try to fake yourself out about the real value this year. It only means that next year you'll have to fake yourself out even more.

	Year	*Other asset value*
1.	_____	_____
2.	_____	_____
3.	_____	_____
4.	_____	_____
5.	_____	_____
6.	_____	_____
7.	_____	_____
8.	_____	_____
9.	_____	_____
10.	_____	_____
11.	_____	_____
12.	_____	_____
13.	_____	_____
14.	_____	_____
15.	_____	_____
Total		_____

Your Insurance in Force Report Card

Dig out the policies. Read them again. List the insurance that's in force right now. It's a great way to make sure that you have all the insurance you need—and of making sure that you're not paying for what you don't need.

Year	*Life policy Number*	*Name of company*	*Amount of Coverage*	*Cash surrender value*	*Premium/monthly or annual*
_____	_____	_____	_____	_____	_____
_____	_____	_____	_____	_____	_____
_____	_____	_____	_____	_____	_____
_____	_____	_____	_____	_____	_____
_____	_____	_____	_____	_____	_____
_____	_____	_____	_____	_____	_____

Year	Disability policy Number	Name of company	Amount of Coverage	Waiting period	Premium/monthly or annual
___	___	___	___	___	___
___	___	___	___	___	___
___	___	___	___	___	___
___	___	___	___	___	___
___	___	___	___	___	___
___	___	___	___	___	___

Your Total Worth Report Card

Assets minus liabilities. It's that simple.

Year	Total Assets	Total Liabilities	Net Worth
___	___	___	___
___	___	___	___
___	___	___	___
___	___	___	___
___	___	___	___
___	___	___	___
___	___	___	___
___	___	___	___
___	___	___	___
___	___	___	___
___	___	___	___
___	___	___	___
Total	___	___	___

Chapter 18

A Word at the End

Every time I give a seminar, people come up to me at the end and ask: "Do you do all the stuff you talk about?" The natural answer is a hearty, ringing, and very sincere "Yes!"

The real answer is … well. After going back over everything that's been tucked in here, I find that I've done about 85-90 percent. I have to admit to owning an expensive car, which I rationalize by telling people it gets me from one meeting to another meeting faster. When I really bought it because it makes me look like Harrison Ford. Exactly like Harrison Ford: don't be fooled by the one could only dream. When I'm behind the wheel of this machine, Harrison Ford and I are identical.

There's some other foolishness I've perpetrated but we don't have any space for it here. If there were space, I'd confess.

Honest. Ask my kids.

But I follow 85-90 percent of my own advice, which is probably a better record than the average high school guidance counsellor, the average stockbroker, or the average diet-book writer.

The result of following my own advice is that I can afford the car that makes me look like Harrison Ford, that I own more of my house than the average individual and will soon own it all, and that I am well ahead on funding my retirement.

I'm 52.

There are few hassles in the house about money. I don't wake up at four in the morning wondering how to cover the credit card bill this month. And I feel a tremendous sense of financial freedom because I have a plan and am sticking to it. And it's working.

I'm not Donald Trump. But, as I pointed out at the beginning, Donald Trump isn't Donald Trump anymore.

It would make me extremely happy if you had a financial plan. And if you stuck to it. And if it worked for you. I hope this book helps you get all that together.

Otherwise it's going to be just Hoskins and me sitting at the end of the dock fishing with just each other to talk to. And I just don't think I could bear listening to him without someone there to share the load.

If you'd like to have a financial plan completed you can email kenneth.wharram@sympatico.ca. You will receive a quote base on a Full, Standard or Simple Plan. Speaking engagements are available for a standard fee plus expenses and can be arranged through the email address above.

978-0-595-51492-2
0-595-51492-8